Out of Fight or Flight

A Journey Through EMDR, Trauma, and the Will to Heal

ZEBULON THOMAS

Out of Fight or Flight

A Journey Through EMDR, Trauma, and the Will to Heal

ZEBULON THOMAS

ISBN: 9798289511409

www.OutofFightorFlight.com

A Note on the Journey

These chapters aren't in order —
because trauma rarely is.

This is how I healed:
one session at a time,
as the body remembered.

That's how you'll walk through this too.

Note to the reader: This book is a personal narrative and does not serve as a substitute for professional medical or mental health advice. The author is not a licensed therapist, and the therapeutic experiences shared are based on personal reflection. If you are struggling with trauma, please seek support from a qualified mental health professional.

For permissions or inquiries, contact:
www.OutofFightorFlight.com
www.ZebulonThomasFilms.com
www.ZebulonThomas.com

Trigger Warning / Content Note

This book includes personal accounts of trauma, including emotional distress, psychological pain, and descriptions of EMDR (Eye Movement Desensitization and Reprocessing) therapy sessions. While every effort has been made to present these experiences responsibly and respectfully, some content may be activating or distressing for readers, especially those with a history of trauma or PTSD.

Please take care of yourself while reading.
You are encouraged to pause, take breaks, and skip sections that feel overwhelming. Healing is not linear, and there is no "right" way to engage with this material.

If at any point you feel unsafe or triggered, consider reaching out to a trusted mental health professional. You are not alone. Support is available.

For immediate help:

- **National Suicide Prevention Lifeline (US):** 988

- **Crisis Text Line (US):** Text HOME to 741741

- **International readers:** Please consult a local emergency resource or mental health organization.

This book is not intended as a substitute for therapy, but as a companion to understanding and honoring the process of healing.

Acknowledgment & Disclaimer

This book is a deeply personal journey through trauma, healing, and survival. It is written from my perspective alone and reflects my experiences and insights.

While I honor and am profoundly grateful to the counselors and mental health professionals who have supported me—whose dedication, compassion, and expertise have been instrumental in my healing—none of them had knowledge of or involvement in the creation of this book. Their participation in my therapy is separate from this work, and this book is not intended as a reflection or commentary on their practices.

This disclaimer is included to respect the privacy and professional boundaries of those who have walked alongside me, and to protect their licenses.

If you are reading this as a survivor or a clinician, please know that this work is meant to offer hope, understanding, and connection. It is not a substitute for professional help.

✧ To the Ones Who Hold the Space

To the counselors and therapists
who walk us through the fire,
who do their own healing to hold ours,
who show up with grace and grit
and sacred steadiness —

You are the miracle
we didn't know we were allowed to ask for.

✦

And to every survivor holding this book —

Know that healing is possible.
That help exists.
And that you are worthy of both.

Dedication

To Fay and Shirley —
I would not be here without you.

That's not just something I say —
it's the deepest truth I carry.

You stepped into the storm with me
when most would have turned away.

You sat in silence
when the weight of my words was too much to speak aloud.

You listened to what I couldn't yet say.
And you waited — patiently —
for the pieces of me to surface,
when even I didn't know they were missing.

You saw through the shaking.
You understood the rage.
You held space when I was unraveling.

And still, you reminded me,
gently and consistently —
*"This is a body remembering.
Let's help it come home."*

Your presence taught me
that healing is not about rushing —
it's about returning.

To breath.
To trust.
To self.

You offered me that sacred return.

Session after session —
without judgment.
Without pressure.

You built a space
where safety could exist —
even when I couldn't feel it yet.

And in that space,
I learned how to feel again.

I know you carry so much
that no one sees.

The weight of clients
who disappeared before the work was done.

The nights you wonder if it mattered.
The heartbreak
of bearing stories
that echo through your bones.

I was one of the ones who stayed.
And because of that — I lived.

If you ever question the impact of your work,
please hear this:

You changed my life.
You helped me reclaim it.

And I survived so I could write this...
Not just for me,
but for the others like me
who still don't have the words.

Thank you.
From the deepest place in me —
thank you.

— Zebulon Thomas

A Note on Style

This book is written in fragments —
short lines, broken sentences, and breath pauses.

It's not a formatting error. It's how trauma speaks.

For years, I didn't have a clear timeline.
I had flashes.
Feelings.
Fragments.

When I began EMDR therapy,
memories surfaced out of order,
emotions rose before language caught up,
and my nervous system spoke in jolts, not paragraphs.

The structure of this book reflects that disorientation —
the way trauma lives in the body
and how healing slowly brings coherence.

You might feel the rhythm shift as you read.
That's intentional.

Some chapters unravel like a storm.
Others steady like a breath.

This is a memoir about healing,
but it's also a mirror —
for anyone whose story doesn't fit neatly on a timeline.

You're not broken. You're remembering.

A Map, If You Need One

Author's Note

Why "Out of Fight or Flight"?

Because some of us lived there for so long, we thought it was normal.
We mistook anxiety for alertness.
We mistook hypervigilance for personality.
We mistook numbness for strength.
We mistook exhaustion for failure.

This book is the moment of waking up from that.
The moment you feel your body unclench for the first time.
The moment you stop preparing for the next hit.
The moment you realize…

you're still here.
Not just alive —
but finally safe enough to heal.

From Me to You

This is not a textbook.
It's not a step-by-step how-to.
It's not even a memoir in the traditional sense.

This is a walk through my healing — in real time.
Through the rooms where I first sat with my trauma.
Through the memories that surfaced during EMDR.
Through the moments I didn't think I'd survive — but did.

Each chapter is one window.
One session.
One turning point.

There will be flashbacks.
Messy details.
There will be moments that might mirror your own.
And moments that might feel completely foreign.

All of it is true.
All of it is mine.
And I offer it to you — *not as advice, but as companionship.*

Whether you're in therapy, avoiding it, searching for it, or standing beside someone who's deep in the work...

I hope this helps you feel less alone.
I hope it helps you understand.
And I hope — if you're ready — it gives you the courage to go in.

Because trauma isn't just what happened.
It's what you had to become to survive it.
This book is about coming back.
— *Zebulon Thomas*

If no one ever told you it was safe to stop running —
let this book be the beginning.

When the Shaking Stopped

There's no way I could tell you everything in this book.
Some stories are still too raw.
Some moments were never meant to be spoken — only survived.

This is not a complete record of my trauma.
It's not a catalog of pain.

It's a journey through what I carried —
and how I finally began to put it down.

I didn't write this book to traumatize anyone.
I don't want you to carry my pain.

But I do hope, somewhere in these pages,
you feel less alone in yours.

I want you to see what trauma can look like.
What it feels like.
How it hides in the body.

How fight or flight becomes the only way to exist —
until, one day, something breaks through.

For me, that breakthrough came with EMDR.

After years of shaking.
Shaking from my core.
Shaking like my nervous system was trapped in a permanent
earthquake —

the trembling finally stopped.

It didn't stop because I ignored it.
It didn't stop because I "got over it."

It stopped because I walked back into the storm —
this time with someone I trusted
to hold the space for me.
To help me stay.
To help me see.

Session after session, I returned to that room.
I cried.
I shook.
I raged.
I came undone.

And still —
my therapist stayed with me.

Held the space.
Never rushed.
Never judged.
Just honored the process, even when I couldn't.

And eventually...
after one of those sessions,

I felt still.
My body didn't tremble.
My heart didn't race.

The earthquake was over.

That stillness was the first time I tasted peace.

I didn't know EMDR would work.
I didn't even know how it worked.
I didn't go home and Google it.
I didn't try to outsmart the process.

I just let it work on me.
Let it do what no other method had ever done.

And the truth is — *it's not magic.*
It's medicine for the parts of the brain trauma tried to shut down.

It's safety that lets the fear finally exit the system.
It's science, yes — but it's also sacred.

This isn't just a story of trauma.
It's a story of processing trauma.
Of choosing to go back into the wreckage and see it through.

It's not easy.

There were days after sessions when I felt rage I didn't understand.
Numbness I couldn't shake.
Overwhelm that made me want to quit.

I call them *EMDR hangovers* — and they're real.

But I didn't stop.
And neither did the healing.

If you're starting EMDR, or thinking about it —
or maybe you quit because it felt like too much —

let me say this with my whole heart:

It's so much harder to live with the trauma
than it is to face it in a safe space
with someone trained to walk beside you.

Let it work.
Give it time.
Let the storm move through you —
and don't run from it this time.

Eventually, the shaking will stop.
And in its place,
there will be a peace you never thought possible.

I was born into trauma.
But I'm not living in it anymore.

⊚ Chapter One

The Buzzers Felt Like Too Much

EMDR Session
The first time I let myself stay

A raging lion.
Fully armored.
Emotionally spent.
Numb. Violent in nature.

That was the shell I had become.

Burned out after a long stretch of success —
creative, relentless.
I gave everything.
Helped others build their empires.
And somewhere in the giving,
I disappeared.

I hit rock bottom.

That's when my wife stepped in.
She booked me a session with a trauma therapist —
someone who used something called EMDR.

I didn't know what that meant.
Didn't care, really.
I had stopped believing anyone could help me.

"They can't change what I went through," I told her.
"They weren't there. No one was."

But I showed up anyway.

The building was familiar —
my accountant's office.
Top floor.

I'd been there for years.
Business meetings. Contracts. Strategy.

Most people took the elevator.
I always took the stairs.

Maybe that should've told me something —
about trust.
About control.

I didn't even realize I was headed to the first floor
until a woman stepped into the waiting room.

She looked at me — not through me.

"Who are you here to see?"

"The EMDR therapist."

She smiled.
"That's me. We'll head downstairs."

She pressed the elevator button.
I froze.

My body said no.
But I smiled. Nodded.
Stepped inside.

I held my fear behind the usual mask.
Smile. Small talk.
Keep the shaking inside.

That's how I survived everything else.

Her office surprised me.
Warm. Lived-in. Not clinical.

There was life here.

Soft light. A couch. Plants.
A framed print about EMDR.
Words that jumped out at me:
Pain. Healing. Release. Awareness.

She let me choose where to sit.
I picked a chair low to the ground.

I told her I had trauma.
That I wasn't sure anything could help.
But I was willing to try.

She didn't flinch.
Didn't say, *"I understand."*

Instead, she handed me two small buzzers.

"Hold these gently in your hands," she said.
"Close your eyes when you're ready.
Just notice what comes up.
I'm right here."

The buzzers began.
Left. Right. Left. Right.

"Take a breath in."

Then:
"Let's create a calm place together.
Somewhere peaceful — just for you.
No one else needs anything from you there."

I pictured a quiet trail I often walk.
Late summer.
A soft river.
Trees swaying gently overhead.

"Good," she said.
"Stay there for a few moments.
Breathe.
You're safe."

It felt like a warm blanket
on a frozen body.

Comforting...
but I still shook inside.

She asked,
"Is there a place you'd like to begin?"

And just like that —
I was in it.

The storm hit fast.

I saw everything.
The beatings.
The kidnapping.
My sister's lips turning blue.
Me — hit by a car.
Me — disappearing into the street.

I saw the house.
The place where fear lived.
And the child I used to be.

Then came rage.
I wanted to fight.
Burn it all.
Watch the flames rise.

"Just stay with what's coming up," she said.
"What do you notice?"

"I want them to feel pain," I said.
"I want parents to burn.
I want to sit in the fire with them —
make sure they're gone."

The buzzers kept going.
Left. Right.

"I want to watch them suffer."

Then she asked — gently:
"Notice what it feels like to be in the fire…
and if there's a part of you that might want to step out."

I froze.

I guess…
I don't have to be there.

"Let's return to your safe place," she said.
"Let yourself land there.
Take your time.
You're safe here.
None of that belongs in this space."

I opened my eyes.
Tears blurred the room.

She met me with soft eye contact —
steady. Present. Unshaken.

I grabbed a tissue.
Sat with the silence.

"I don't know what that was," I finally said.
"But… wow."

"It's powerful," she said softly.
"Welcome to EMDR.
I think we've got some work to do."

I nodded.
Still unsure.
Still scared.

But something in me knew:
I would come back.

✿ Closing Reflection

That day, I learned
I don't need to burn with them.
I don't need to sit in the fire
to prove what they did to me.

I'm not ready to forgive.
But I'm ready to face it.

That moment —
when I didn't run,
when I stayed —
was the beginning.

Not to be fixed,
but to begin healing.

When I left her office,
she said gently:
"I hope to see you next week.
It's going to be hard.
But you're going to learn how to process all of this —
and eventually… you'll heal."

❖A Question to Sit With
What if healing doesn't mean forgetting —
but finally letting your body know
it can stop carrying what happened?

✧ ECHOES

The Fire Was Never Mine

When I got home from that first session,
I didn't say much.
Not right away.

The buzzers were still echoing in my body.
My chest buzzed.
My hands tingled.
The images kept looping —
not like memories,
but like ghosts that hadn't finished with me yet.

My wife asked how it went.
I opened my mouth…
but the words didn't feel big enough.

How do you explain what it means
to stand inside the fire —
and choose to stay?

That session was the first time
I didn't run.
Didn't freeze.
Didn't leave my body behind.

I stayed.
Not in the trauma —
but in the room.
In myself.
In the truth.

I've spent decades building armor.
A warrior.
A fighter.
A survivor.

But the buzzers did something I didn't expect.
They bypassed the warrior
and found the boy.

The boy who still lives inside me.
And he's scared.

That night, I felt raw.
Agitated.
Tired but wired.
Like the session had torn something open
and left it exposed.

No one tells you about the first night.
The emotional hangover.
How the storm doesn't end
when the session ends.

It lingers.
It sharpens.
It scrapes the inside of your ribs.

I bounced between sadness,
grief,
rage.

The anger surged like a wave I couldn't ride.
All I saw was red —
red like my mother's fists.
Red like the fire I wanted to burn it all down with.

My therapist had mentioned to me,
softly:

"This might come up.
Let it.
Sit with the feelings.
Don't grip them.
Don't fix.
Just feel.
And avoid the things that block the flow —
caffeine, sugar,

anything that numbs or heightens.
Your brain will keep processing for 24 to 48 hours.
Let it do the work."

So I didn't run.
I didn't drink.
I didn't try to make it go away.

I just cried.
I sat on the floor and let it come.

Because that night,
the lion in me —
the one who had roared for years just to survive —
finally stopped pacing.

And for the first time,
he didn't need to fight.

He just needed to be seen.
To rest.
To know that healing was possible.

And maybe — just maybe —
he had found the right place to begin.

Chapter Two
Before the Storm

EMDR Session
Naming what I thought was just "life"

I'm not telling this part in order —
because it didn't happen in order inside me.
This is just how it lives.
How it surfaced.

Before the first memory came up in therapy —
before the bench,
before the tears —
there was the storm I lived in every day
but didn't know had a name.

I called it being driven.
I called it hard work.
I called it being on guard.

But it was trauma.
Wearing armor.
Living in survival mode.

I never walked into a room
without scanning the exits.
Never sat with my back to a crowd.
Never fully trusted anyone —
not with my back,
not with my story,
not with my heart.

I didn't know my brain was working overtime —
rehearsing worst-case scenarios,
flashing images
of everything that could go wrong
as if it already had.

And my body?
It believed every single one.

My chest stayed tight.
My breath never dropped low.
My jaw was clenched for so long
I forgot what it meant
to feel relaxed.

I looked calm.
Successful, even.

But inside…
I was a battlefield.

I wasn't chasing dreams —
I was chasing safety.
And I mistook survival
for purpose.

People praised my ambition.
They saw the talent,
the drive,
the work ethic.

But none of it came from peace.
It came from trying to stay alive.

I emancipated myself at sixteen.
I had had enough.

The court case dragged.
Three months
in juvenile detention
while it played out —
fighting off kids
bigger, harder, meaner.

Trying to survive again,
even though all I wanted
was to be free.

To be safe.

I won.

But before all that —
before the court —
we moved in with my grandfather.

Our landlord was selling the house.
We needed somewhere to go.

My grandmother had MS.
The plan was to help care for her
while we got back on our feet.

It was supposed to be a new beginning.

But it didn't take long
for the fighting to start.

My father and grandfather —
his father —
went at it daily.

Screaming.
Accusations.
Doors slamming.

The energy in that house
got darker by the week.

And eventually,
it exploded.

My grandfather gave us no choice.
He forced us out.

Not because he didn't care
about me, my brother, my sister —
but because he couldn't take the chaos anymore.

My dad had become too toxic.
The house wasn't safe
for anyone.

So we lost another home.

And I lost more than just a roof.

I lost what little hope I had
that adults could be steady.
That family could be safe.
That maybe this time,
we'd be okay.

In 1999, they said the world would end.
That Y2K would crash everything.

But it wasn't the computers I feared.

I'd grown up hearing Jesus was coming back —
that the earth would be taken,
and the ones left behind would suffer.

I didn't understand religion.
But I believed it.
And I was terrified.

Still in high school.
Barely.

Already moved too many times —
three towns,
four schools.

In 8th grade,
we lived in a van.

The school bus dropped me down the street.
I walked the rest of the way
and called it home.

And somehow…
it was still my fault.

That's what they told me.
That I was the reason we had nothing.

After emancipation,
I found the streets.

Started running with dangerous people —
outlaws, killers, drug dealers,
men who smiled
with knives in their pockets.

I wasn't just a kid with trauma anymore.
I was walking the edge
of something dark.

Getting pulled into a life
that could've swallowed me whole.

I almost got caught up for real.
Almost became another statistic.

I saw things
no one should see.
Things I'll never say out loud.

And somehow —
I came out without a criminal record.
No addictions.
No permanent stain on my name.

Not because I was lucky.

Because I met her.

My wife.

She pulled me out
before it was too late.

Spent time with me.
Showed me how to laugh.
How to do normal things.

How to feel safe
without a weapon in my hand.

She showed me I could be more.
That I didn't have to go out in a blaze —
I could just live.

I made friends,
but I didn't keep them.

Turned friendships into business deals —
because business felt safer
than connection.

I believed people didn't want me —
they wanted what I could create.

So I built walls.
Said no to going out.
Kept people at a distance.

Other times,
I went wild —
partying, chasing intensity,
living without fear.

The highs were manic.
The lows felt like drowning.

It wasn't bipolar.

It was trauma.

I was also searching —
for touch,
for love,
for safety in someone's arms.

And somehow,
I found it in her.

We were both running from abuse.
And we found each other
in the middle of that escape.

We built something together —
a bond.
A family.
A safe place.

But even that wasn't untouched.

She saw the breakdowns.
The anger.
The rants.

She feared what I might do —
to myself,
or to someone who hurt me.

Still,
I never broke our bond.

Our relationship was — and is — abuse-free.
It's the only thing I fully trust.

But my trauma still spilled over.

In words.
In tension.
In the fear I carried
into every room
we walked into together.

At work,
I became unstoppable.

Outperformed people with degrees.
With decades of experience.

Did the impossible —
again and again.

Why?
Because I had no choice.
Because I was still surviving.

They gave me pressure —
I gave results.
They handed me chaos —
I built systems.

I learned fast.

Created jobs.
Faced fears
just to not be left behind.

I was afraid of rejection —
so I overachieved.

But even then,
they used me.

Used my ideas.
My time.
My talent.

And when they were done —
they didn't just walk away.
They emptied me.

Took what they needed.
Left my name off the credits.
Pretended I was never part of the build.

They got the glory.
I got the burnout.

And because I was good at hiding pain
behind performance,
they never saw what it cost me.

But I did.
And it almost broke me.

🌿 Closing Reflection

I didn't know what to call it back then —
hypervigilance, survival mode, fight or flight.
Those were just words I hadn't learned yet.

I thought I was wired differently —
intense, focused, unstoppable.

But therapy gave language
to what I'd lived.

Once it had a name,
it was harder to pretend it wasn't real.

This session wasn't about one memory.
It was about the operating system
I ran on for decades —

The armor I called ambition.
The panic I called drive.
The exhaustion I thought was just life.

I used to scan every room for exits.
Sometimes I still do.
But now, I understand why.

This is what EMDR began to unravel —
not just memories, but patterns.
Not just flashbacks,
but the framework my life was built on.

And it's unsettling.

Because when I look back
at the years I was celebrated the most —
those were the years I was surviving the hardest.

The trauma never stopped me.
But it did shape me.

And now,
I'm slowly unlearning
how to live like the storm
is still coming.

❖**A Question to Sit With**
What if the life you called "normal" —
was actually your body's way
of keeping you alive?

What would it mean
to stop surviving
and start healing?

✧ ECHOES

Naming the Storm

The second session hit harder.
I thought I knew what I was carrying.

But once we started —
once the buzzers began —
the memories didn't just return...
they surged.

Flashbacks.
Buried images.
Heat and fire
under my skin.

Pain I thought I'd already learned to live with —
but had never truly faced.

I didn't like how it felt.
Not because it was wrong...
but because it was real.

No more armor.
Just rawness.
Exposed nerves.

The rage in me was louder than the grief —
and it didn't want to sit still.

I paced the house that night
like a caged animal.

Everything in me was awake —
but not settled.

It wasn't just emotional.
It was somatic.
My body held the storm,
and now it was trying to release it.

My therapist had explained to me this could happen.
That emotions might swing.
That I might feel more vulnerable —
or more agitated.

That crying might not come right away —
and that's okay.

To let the body lead.
To not force it.
Not numb it.

Just allow.

No stimulants.
No distractions.

Just rest.
Hydration.
Awareness.

So I slept.
Hard.
Over twelve hours.

The next day, I couldn't do much.
I didn't want to.

I was emotionally offline.
Still rewiring.
Still in the aftershocks
of everything we stirred up.

But one thing surprised me:
I wanted to go back.

Even in the discomfort —
maybe because of it —

something in me was ready.
Ready to keep going.
To face what had chased me.

To keep naming it.
To keep holding the buzzers.
And to see where it would take me next.

Chapter Three

No One Came Looking

EMDR Session
When going back felt safer than being gone

I don't remember exactly
what my therapist said that day.
But I remember what she created:
Space.
Stillness.
A place I could enter the storm
and not face it alone.

The buzzers started.
Left. Right. Left. Right.
I dropped in.

This time,
I thought I was ready.
But I wasn't ready
for what surfaced.

I saw myself —
a little boy,
on the floor,
playing.

Just being a kid.

Then suddenly,
I was yanked up by the arm.

Earlier that day,
I had tried to reach a box of cereal.
In the process,
I knocked over a drinking bird —
a glass toy filled with blue dye

that tipped and rocked when it moved.

It was a gift.
Something new.
Something she cared about.

It fell off the counter.
Shattered.
Blue dye spilled across the white tile.

It was everywhere.

I panicked.
Tried to clean it up.
Swept the glass,
threw it away,
wiped the floor.

But the stain remained.

Hours passed.
Then she found it.

She asked if I broke it.
I told her the truth.
I said yes.

She screamed.
She hit me.
She said I ruined everything.
That I made her hurt me.
That it was my fault.
That I'd never be forgiven.

That she'd never let me forget.

She beat me
until I couldn't see
through the tears.

Then she grabbed the back of my neck
and threw me into my room.

My face hit the carpet.
I slid —
into my toys,
to the foot of my bed.

I crawled under the blankets
and cried.

She slammed the door.
Left the lights off.
Told my brother
not to check on me.

She never came back.

After what felt like hours,
I grabbed my stuffed animal,
opened the window,
and ran.

Into the woods.
Nowhere in mind —
I just wanted away.

I felt unwanted.
Unloved.
Like I didn't belong
in that house.

The woods were terrifying.
But somehow,
they felt safer than home.

I climbed a tree —
higher than I ever had.
High enough
to see over rooftops.

To see my house.
The edge of town.

The sun was setting.
The sky was glowing.

Everything looked peaceful.

But I didn't feel peaceful.
I felt broken.

I remember thinking:
Why is life like this?
Why do my parents hurt me?
Is this normal?

I was eight.

The abuse had started
years before that —
but I didn't have words yet.
I just thought I was bad.
That I was the problem.

I stayed in that tree
until dark.
Cold.
Crying.
Waiting.

But no one came.
No one looked.
No one called my name.

Eventually,
I climbed down.
I couldn't get back in
through the window,
so I walked around the house
and slipped through the side door
into the garage.

She was in the kitchen —
on the phone.

She didn't look surprised.
Didn't ask where I'd been.
Didn't ask if I was okay.

She just pointed to the door.
Motioned for me to go back outside.

No words.
Just dismissal.

I stood there —
frozen, confused,
trying not to cry.

Then she walked over,
opened the door,
and shoved me out.

The door slammed shut.

I turned,
pressed my face to the window.
She walked over
and closed the curtain.

Sealing me out
like I was nothing.

I was cold.
Terrified.
Still clutching my stuffed animal
like it was the only thing I had left.

I sat on the porch.
I didn't know what else to do.

I was too afraid to leave,
but more afraid to be left.

I cried
until my body ached.
Until the tears ran dry.

And still—
no one came.
No one looked.
No one called.

Eventually,
I tried the door again.
It wasn't locked.

I slipped inside.
Quiet.

The kitchen was empty now.
The bathroom light was on.
A faint glow under the door.

I crept down the hallway,
step by step,
careful not to make a sound.

At my bedroom door,
I turned the handle
slowly.

My brother was sleeping.

I didn't wake him.
Didn't want him to see me like that.
Didn't want him to ask
questions I couldn't answer.

Didn't want him to get hurt, too.

I crawled into bed.
Same clothes.
Still shaking.
Still crying,
quietly.

We had school in the morning.

And somehow —
I was glad.

School meant escape.
Away from the yelling.
The hitting.
Her.

Home was the danger.
School was the break.

Even if no one knew.
Even if I had to pretend
nothing was wrong.

That night,
I didn't sleep much.

But I survived it.
And that had to be enough.

Then my therapist said softly,
"Okay... come back to your safe place."

I was still holding the buzzers.
Still inside the dark.
Still in that memory.

But I shifted.

I went there —
to the river.

The light through the trees.
The wind on my face.

That was my place.
Not imagined—real.

A place I'd been.
A place where time stood still.
Where the world softened.
Where peace felt possible,
even when the storm rose up.

I stayed there.
I breathed.

I didn't rush to leave.
My body was still holding so much.

But the water,
the trees,
the quiet —
they held me too.

When I was ready,
I opened my eyes.

She was still there.

Still present.
Still steady.

Not waiting for words.
Just holding space.
Letting me land.

She didn't ask me to explain.
She didn't need to.

She let the silence do the work.

She let me feel it all.

And in that quiet,
after everything I had walked through,
I realized:

This —
this is what it means to feel safe.
To be seen.
To be believed.

Maybe for the first time.

🌿 Closing Reflection

For so long,
I thought safety was impossible.

When I ran,
I wasn't just trying to escape what was happening —
I was trying to find something else.

But I didn't know what "else" was.

The yard.
The woods.
That was as far as I'd ever gone.

Beyond that felt terrifying —
like a point of no return.

Still,
I kept hoping someone would come looking.
That someone would miss me.
Wonder if I was okay.
Worry for my safety.

But no one did.

And for a long time,
I didn't understand
why I went back.

Back to the danger.
Back to her.

But I'm learning.

And slowly,

I'm letting myself open.

❖A Question to Sit With
What would it feel like to believe —
even for a moment —
that you deserve to be safe?

Not because someone else says you are,
but because you hold that space for yourself.

✧ ECHOES

The Storm After the Storm

I didn't go straight home.
I couldn't.

I was still shaking —
from everything that had been stirred up —
yet inside, there was stillness too.

The kind that comes after chaos.
The kind I remember from childhood.

When the beatings stopped.
When the yelling died down.
When the door slammed shut.

And I was left frozen, alone.

That's what this felt like.

My legs were heavy.
My eyes burned.
My head buzzed with everything I didn't —
or couldn't —
say out loud.

It was quiet,
but the memories flashed like lightning.

EMDR doesn't always feel like healing when it ends.
Sometimes it feels like breaking.

I sat in my car for twenty minutes.
Not driving.
Not talking.
Just… existing.

The world outside kept moving —
accountants walking into offices,

other survivors passing through the doors,
cars pushing forward like nothing had happened.

But inside,
time had stalled.

I felt emptied.
Like something had been torn loose
and left a hollow space behind.

I didn't cry right away.
That came later.
On the drive.

Then it would stop.
Then come again —
a deep emotional flood
with no shape, no words.

I stopped at a quiet park.

It was cold.
Raining.
Empty.

No people.
No noise.

I walked a slow lap around the trail —
the same one I used in my Safe Place.

I could feel everything.
Too much.

My skin was loud.
My breath, shallow.

My body wasn't sure if I was safe.

It reminded me of childhood —
the times I got beat
and walked into the woods after,

even in the middle of winter,
cold and wet like this.

What helped:
– Quiet
– Wind
– Letting myself feel strange without judging it
– Talking to no one

What didn't help:
– Thinking I should be "over it"
– Pretending I was okay
– Telling myself it wasn't a big deal
– Acting like this kind of abuse was normal
– Minimizing it because I had survived worse
– Comparing my pain to someone else's
– Trying to move on instead of moving through

And maybe the hardest part?
Knowing that if I told someone what I had just faced in that session,
they might not understand.

They might flinch.
Or freeze.
Or say too much.
Or say nothing at all.

So I stayed quiet.

But I stayed with it.

Because this pain wasn't just something that happened.
It was still happening —

in my body,
in my breath,
in the parts of me that had waited years to be held,
seen,
believed.

This wasn't release.
Not yet.

This was the storm after the storm.

And somehow...
I stayed with it.

I didn't run.
I didn't shut it down.

I let the silence wrap around me like a coat
I didn't ask for —
but needed to wear
until I could set it down for good.

That day, I knew:
I had to go back.

To the chair.
To the paddles.
To the parts of me I hadn't seen in decades.

Not to suffer.
But to rescue what had been lost.

Because if I was willing to walk back into the storm...
I might finally walk myself out of it.

Chapter Four

He Didn't Run

EMDR Session
Sitting beside the child I thought I'd lost

The room was quiet.
Just me and her.

I wrapped my fingers around the buzzers—familiar now, not so terrifying.
The hum began.
Left. Right. Left. Right.

She said,
"Let's sit with him today."

And just like that,
I was back in it—
not in the chaos,
but in something deeper.

I saw the bench.
The woods.
The boy.

And I walked toward the part of me I lost long ago.

This was the session that cracked something open in me.
So deep, so consuming—
I couldn't even speak afterward.
My body was shaking.
My face wet.
I felt hollow and awake all at once,
like I had just survived a spiritual surgery.

In that memory,
I saw the boy.

Five years old.
Small legs swinging over the edge of the bench,
looking out toward the trees.

He didn't turn around.
But he knew.
He felt me.

I sat down slowly beside him.

He didn't look at me—
just kept swinging his feet,
barely brushing the leaves below.

I stared at him—at me.
I could see it all…
what he had already survived,
what was coming.
The moments that would break him.
The pain that would take his innocence.
The day I would lose him completely—
the day the storm took him.

My chest tightened.
The grief came in a wave.

Then my therapist's voice cut through the fog, calm and steady:
"Who else is here with you and the boy?"

And just like that,
I saw him—
the protector.

He stood in the distance,
quiet but watchful.
Not a monster. Not a shadow.
A presence.

"What do you notice about that part?" she asked gently.
"Is this maybe where that protector showed up?"

I nodded.
My eyes were still locked on the boy.

But I could feel it—
the way I had created someone fierce
to stand guard for the one who was helpless.

She asked,
"What does he need?"
"What do you want him to know?"

I hesitated.
"I didn't like him," I said.
"He was violent. Full of rage."

"And what's that rage protecting?" she asked softly.

I swallowed.
Tears pooled again.

"Me," I said.
"That little boy.
It's how he fought to keep us safe."

"Could that part be misunderstood?"

I nodded slowly.
I was starting to see it—
see *him*.
Understand where he came from.
What he had done for us.

I didn't like him.
But I knew I needed to meet him.
Sit with him.
Forgive him.
Thank him.
Or maybe just accept him.

I wasn't just sitting with the boy anymore.
There were three of us now—
all versions of me.
Each carrying something vital.
Each shaped by survival.

Then my therapist's voice anchored me again:

"What do you want to say to the boy?"
"Let him know."

I took in a shaky breath.
Then said it aloud:

"Run."
"Run away. Leave. Don't look back. Someone will find you.
Someone will love you and protect you and give you the life you
deserve.
This is your only chance. Please… escape."

For a long moment, he didn't move.

Then, slowly,
the little boy turned toward me.

He looked me in the eye and said,

"It's okay. I'll be okay.
I have you now.
You'll walk with me."

That moment never really ended.
It became part of me.

I didn't just meet my inner child that day—
I listened to him.
I saw him choose to stay.

And in doing so,
I realized something:

I wasn't broken.
I was brave.

The storm didn't take him.
He waited for me to come back.
And now…
I walk with him.

After that session,
I could barely stand.

My therapist suggested I step outside—
there was a small patch of woods and meadow behind the
building.

I nodded, grabbed my things, and wandered there without a word.
I stayed in those trees for 45 minutes.
Crying.
Breathing.
Grieving.
Releasing everything I had just remembered...
and everything I finally couldn't carry anymore.

It was surreal—
those woods looked exactly like the ones I played in as a child.
The same overgrown trails.
The same light through the leaves.
It felt like I had returned to the place I disappeared from.

🌿 Closing Reflection

That day, I saw all of me.
Not just the pain—
but the protector, too.
The one who fought.
The one who stayed.
The one who waited for me to come back.

For so long, I thought survival made me broken.

But now I see—

it made me whole.

❖A Question to Sit With
If you could sit beside your younger self—
in a quiet moment, like on that bench—
what would you say to them?

What do you wish they had known?
And what do you most need to hear now?

✧ ECHOES
The Woods Didn't Let Go Right Away

I stayed out there longer than I meant to.
In the trees.
In the silence.
In the grief.

It didn't feel like I was walking away from something.
It felt like something was still holding me.

Not the memory —
but the weight of finally feeling it.

The woods behind the building reminded me of the ones I used to
run to
after the beatings.
Same look.
Same sound.
Same quiet.

Only this time,
I wasn't hiding.
I was facing it.

The observer.
Processing.
Grieving.

I felt so incredibly grateful in that moment
that my therapist had suggested I take time back there.

As if she had used that place herself.
As if she knew —

I needed grounding.
I needed stillness.
And I couldn't create it on my own.

Her timing was perfect.
I couldn't have processed this on the road.

She knew that.
She gave me something
I didn't know how to ask for.

I don't remember much of the drive home.
I was blurry.
Heavy.
Exhausted in a way sleep wouldn't fix.

When I walked into the house,
I didn't talk.
I didn't sit at the table.
I paced.

My wife looked at me and knew —
this wasn't just a hard session.
This was a fracture
that had finally been touched.

Then I crashed on the couch.
Two hours of deep sleep.
Grief sleep.

I cried again that night.
Not in a dramatic way.
It just kept leaking out.

Like my body hadn't gotten the message
that the storm had passed.

The next morning,
I felt like I had the flu.
EMDR hangover.

The kind where your skin aches,
your eyes won't focus.
Where silence is too loud,
and noise is unbearable.

Everything felt open.
Everything felt tender.

I couldn't think.
Only feel.

But something was different.
I didn't feel afraid of the next session.
I felt... called.

Like the five-year-old me had handed me something —
not just his trust,
but a quiet strength I didn't know I still carried.

He didn't ask me to fix anything.
He didn't demand justice.

He just looked at me and said,
**"I have you now.
Thank you for coming back for me."**

And that changed everything.

Because for the first time,
I wasn't going back to EMDR to break apart.

I was going back to walk with him —
to help him carry the pieces,
instead of leaving him behind in the ruins.

But there was another part of me
I still had to face.

The protector.
The one who sat on the bench too —
wearing the armor.

All the weight.
The arrows in my back.
The scars.
The bloodstains.

I had become the wall.
The barrier.
The shield that blocked the worst of the trauma
from reaching him.

And I didn't like him.
Not at first.

This was the version of me
who walked into that office on day one —
hard,
guarded,
worn.

But I think I'm starting to understand him.

Who he is.
Why he exists.
What he's carried for us.

The years of abuse.
The layers of survival.
All the ages.
All the stages.

This wasn't just one wound.
This was C-PTSD —
trauma compounded over time.

It didn't make the next day easier.
I still felt wrecked.
Tender.
Like every nerve was awake and shivering.

But underneath the exhaustion,
there was something steady.

Something like peace.

Maybe not healing yet...
but direction.

And that was enough to keep going.

I needed to go back.
To be in that room.
With her.
Holding those buzzers.
Going into the storm.

⌾ Chapter Five

The Day Everything Broke

EMDR Session
Walking Through the Fire That Never Went Out

She sits across from me and hands me the buzzers.
"We can go straight in if you're ready," she says.
"You don't need the safe place first unless you want to."

We had already talked about where my head was that day.
She knew I needed to go straight into the storm.

The buzzers begin — left, right, left.
Immediately, I'm there.
Back in that terrifying moment.
That very scary place that runs rampant in my nervous system, my mind, my body.

Fear.
Anxiety.

I take a deep breath — but it's cut short.
I flutter.
I stumble.
I tremble.
I squeeze the buzzers so hard I almost break them.

I get stuck.
Freeze.
Fight or flight ramps up.
All the emotions hit me at once.

I start to speak.
I tell her what I'm seeing, what I'm remembering, what I'm experiencing.

I was 14 years old.

It was the day I came home from school.
Got off the bus.
Walking down to the house we lived in with my grandfather at the time.

I walked inside and knew something was off.
Something didn't feel right.

My brother ran up to me, breathless.
Dad and grandpa — his dad — were fighting.

I ran to the living room.
I saw my dad holding my grandfather by the throat against the refrigerator.

To my left was my grandmother, in her wheelchair, screaming for my dad to stop choking him.

My grandfather — between breaths, when he could speak —
would yell at my dad to finish him. To do it.
Challenging him.

The hatred between them was a storm I couldn't understand.
I couldn't tell who was right or wrong.
All I knew was I hated seeing my grandfather being choked by my father.

I pleaded with my dad to stop.
He wouldn't even look at me.
His eyes locked on my grandfather's, screaming he was going to kill him.

My grandmother kept screaming.
My brother and I were crying, telling him to stop.

And then — finally — it was over.
My dad let go.
My grandfather collapsed to the floor, coughing and gasping as he tried to regain his breath.

He walked over to my grandmother and told her to shut up.
Called her terrible names.
Pushed her over in her wheelchair.

She fell out and lay on the floor.

Then my dad ran out of the house.
We followed outside.
He was gone.
He ran into the woods.

My mom chased after him but lost him.
She came back, grabbed my sister, and we all jumped into the van.

She drove us to a neighbor's house and left us there.
Then she made calls — friends, family — trying to find my dad.

Hours later, my brother went looking for him with my mom,
leaving me with my sister.

They came back without him but said he was sitting by a tree.
Sitting, staring out into a field.
Crying.
Emotionally drained.
Lost in his gaze.

I was frightened.
Scared.
Not knowing what would happen next.

My brother said my dad might try to kill himself.
And suddenly, the fear of losing him flooded through my nervous
system.

I didn't understand why I was so afraid to lose him.
After everything.
After the mental abuse.
The beatings.
The chaos.

But fear doesn't wait for logic.

That night, something inside me shattered.
My body began to shake uncontrollably — down to my bones.
A nervous breakdown, I called it.

I felt like I wanted to throw up.

I couldn't eat.

I went to school afraid of everything.
Every loud noise.
Every ringing bell.
Teachers coming up behind me.

I couldn't focus.
I was trembling inside, terrified — not knowing what I would find when I got home.

The school bus dropped me off at my grandfather's house.
But I couldn't go home there anymore.
We were kicked out.
Not allowed back.

So I had to walk four doors down on the countryside — about a mile — to a neighbor's house.
A place where I was allowed to stay, to get warm, eat some food, use the bathroom, shower, and clean up.

And then, back to the van where we slept until we found a new place.
That van felt like a prison.
Coming and going to school felt humiliating.

But at school — that became my new home.
A place where I felt safe.
Warm meals.
Friends.
Normality.

No chaos.
No strange times.
No fear.
No overwhelm.

Even though I shook inside.
Not knowing what the future held.
Not knowing what I would face when I came home.

I remember going back to my grandfather's to get the rest of my

things.
Packing up what little I had left.

Another fight happened that day.
Just as bad.
Lasted an hour.

My mom and dad teaming up on my grandfather.
Yelling.
Throwing things.
Pushing him around.
Raging.

My grandfather didn't fight back.
Didn't speak.
Just tried to escape.
To be invisible.
To not be a part of their cruelty.

He tried to disappear.
To fold himself into the corner of the room.
To vanish like smoke.

But my parents wouldn't let him.
They cornered him.
Blocked the door.
Told him terrible things —

"You should kill yourself."

My dad said if he did, he wouldn't clean him up.
He'd leave him in the backyard.
For the animals to eat.

Those words cut deep.
Not just in my mind —
but seared into my nervous system.

That fight ended differently.
My mom ran out of the house —
With a handgun.

I chased after her into the woods.

She was yelling she was going to kill herself.

I begged her to stop.
Screamed.
Pleading.
"Mom, I love you. Please, I need you. We need you."

She turned and said if I took a step closer, she would shoot.
I took a step forward.
She fired two shots.

I froze.
She missed.
I don't know how.
Something was watching over me.

I was terrified.
In shock.
She ran off.
Never looked back.
Nothing.

In that EMDR session, this part of the trauma didn't register.
No feelings.
No memories.
Just blankness.

I should have been overwhelmed.
Afraid.
Crying.
Angry.

But there was nothing.
Numbness.

Holding the buzzers, they shook me.
Pulled everything out.
But this moment was hollow.
Like the gunshots blasted all emotional anchors away.

I'd never experienced that before.
No feeling.

A blank space in my trauma.

My mom shooting at me —
Everything changed in that moment.

Maybe my nervous system protected me,
saying it was too much to bear.
I don't know.

But I am processing it now.

Tears fall from my face in the storm.
I rage.
Hatred I've never felt before.

I squeeze the buzzers as they change vibration and intensity.
My grip tightens like never before.
In the back of my mind, I fear I might break them.

My therapist's voice is soft.
"You're here now. I'm right here with you."

She creates space for me.

The rage pours out.
I speak it aloud.
I want to kill them both.
Choke the life from them.
Show them how much pain I carry.

But I know no amount of violence could ever cause the pain they
gave me.
They will never feel what I have lived through.

I feel monstrous.
A beast.
I want to destroy everything.

And then I realize —
I don't have to perish with them.

I have a choice.
I can walk away.

I am here.
In the storm.
Facing it.
Not then — now.
Bigger.
Wiser.
Stronger.

I survived.

But the weight still lingers.
It plays in my head like it's happening right now.
So real.
All I can do is release it.

Tears.
Breaths.
Grief.
Sobs.

My therapist's voice calls softly.
"When you're ready, return to your safe place."

I go back.
My safe place feels different.
I see the sun.
The leaves.
The river flowing.
I hear it all.
It calms me.

But I'm still shaking.
Vibrating.
Breathing hard.
Like I just left a battlefield.

Trying to pull myself together.
Look back on what just happened.

When I turn around, the portal closes.
There is no past.
No future.

Just present.

I realize I am safe.
I breathe in.
I open my eyes.

My therapist sits across from me, holding space.
Silence.
I wipe tears from my face.
Look at her.
Look down.
Break down again.

She just holds space.
Allows me to feel what I buried.

🌿 Closing Reflection

I remember feeling frustrated—
not with my therapist,
not with EMDR,
but with myself.

Parts of that trauma didn't register—
even though they should have.
The impact was there,
but I was numb, unable to explain.

Everything else unlocked doors,
allowed me to flow,
to feel,
to process.

But this spot was a blank.

And I still don't understand why.

❖A Question to Sit With
What part of your pain are you still trying to outrun,
and what might happen if someone simply sat with you in it?

✧ ECHOES

Held in the Storm

The storm doesn't always roar.
Sometimes it whispers in the quiet places —
after the buzzers stop,
after the sobbing ends,
after I sit in the car, staring at nothing,
trying to remember how to be human again.

That night, I didn't sleep.
The next day, I was full of rage.

Everything felt too tight.
Too loud.
Too heavy in my skin.

And still —
I didn't shut it down.
Didn't bury it.
Didn't channel it elsewhere.

I let myself feel.

Even when it burned.
Even when it made no sense.

That's what healing asks of you.
Not perfection —
presence.
permission.
practice.

And in that room,
with my fingers wrapped around the buzzers,
I unraveled a memory so loud
it had swallowed decades of my life.

She didn't flinch.

My therapist didn't rush to fix it,
or quiet the thunder.

She made space for the storm.
Let it rise.
Let me shake.
Let me hate.
Let me be there
until I didn't have to be anymore.

And when I couldn't breathe,
she didn't try to stop it.
Didn't pull me out.

She stayed with me in it.

Her silence said what words couldn't.
Her steadiness reminded me:
I was no longer alone.

This is the sacred work of trauma healing —
the unseen victories.
the soft unravelings.
the truth that even in your darkest memory,
if you stay long enough,
the light eventually finds its way in.

🌀 Chapter Six
The Protector Within

EMDR Session
From Hate to Understanding — Meeting the Guardian I Never Wanted

**"Okay, let's go to your safe place.
Spend some time there."** my therapist said softly.

I grabbed the buzzers.
Left. Right.
Left. Right.
This time,
I drifted into my safe place
more gently.
The quiet before the storm.

I spent some time here —
calm,
accepting,
thinking about the little boy I met on the bench.

My younger self.
Still innocent.
Still intact.
Still unbroken.

He had experienced trauma —
but not like the older version of me.

And after a few deep breaths,
a few quiet moments of peace,
my therapist spoke gently,

**"Let's check in with your younger self again.
Just notice what shows up.
If someone's there, see if anything stands out about them —**

**what they look like, what they're doing.
What do you notice?"**

The buzzers picked up speed.
The rhythm in my hands
matched the rhythm in my chest.
Buzzing.
Pulsing.
Building.

And then—

I fell.

It was still.
It was silent.

But in the silence,
I saw him.

The monster.
The one I believed I was.
Full of violence.
Full of anger.
A beast born of pain.
Claws sharp.
Teeth bared.
Eyes wild.

The lion.
The raging fire.
The revenge.

The need for justice —
so old, so deep —
it was like it had always been there.

But underneath all of that...
I started to understand.

He wasn't a monster.
He wasn't bad.

He was there
because I needed him.
I created him.

At six years old.
When it got really, really bad —
he arrived.

To protect me.
To take the blows.
To block the words.
To deflect the arrows.
To carry the weight.

He didn't know how to cry.
He only knew how to endure.

And I hated him for that.

But now —
I saw him.

He wasn't this raging lion.

He was the little boy
in armor
too heavy for his small frame.

An attic formed in my mind —
dim, dusty, packed.
Box after box of trauma.
Locked trunks of memories.
Drawers full of secrets.
Doors I had welded shut.

And there —
standing in front of it all —
was the protector.

Hands on every door.
Foot over every crack.
Holding it all together.
Pushing it back.

It's quiet here.
It's lonely.
But it's controlled.

Because I know where everything is.
I know what must never be touched.
What must never get out.

I've labeled every box with silence.
Bound each memory with fear.

And I stand here —
not as a victim —
but as the gatekeeper.

Because someone has to do it.
Because someone had to survive it.

He — the protector —
wasn't built from hate.
He was built
from necessity.

He doesn't smile.
He doesn't cry.
He holds.
He absorbs.
He shields.

He's made of muscle and fury,
but underneath,
he's just a child
who was never allowed to be one.

And in this moment —
as the tears blur my vision —
I see him clearly.

Not as a monster.
Not as a threat.
But as a boy
who put on armor

too big for his frame
and wore it anyway.

He didn't ask to be strong.
He just needed to be.
Because no one else showed up.

And so,
he stayed.

And now —
he's tired.

He wants to put it down.
But he doesn't know how.
And he's afraid.

Because if he's not protecting…
what is he?
Does he even have a purpose without the pain?

That's when I realize —
I can give him a new role.

He can stay,
but not as the shield.
Not as the sword.

He can stay as
companion.
As witness.
As me.

And in my mind —
I bring us together.
Me.
My protector.
The little boy on the bench.

We sit beside one another.
Shoulder to shoulder.
And we hug.

I'm on the right.
The boy is on the left.
The protector is in the middle.

We honor him.
We thank him.
We love him.

"You can set the armor down," I say.

I cry.
I cry so hard,
it feels like my body is purging.

My therapist holds space.
She's silent.
Letting me unravel.

And when I finally catch my breath,
she speaks —

**"Good.
When you're ready, bring yourself back to your safe place.
You can bring those parts with you if it feels right."**

And that—
that breaks me.

Because I can.

I can bring them.

We walk together —
me, the child, the protector —
into the safe place.

It's warm here.
Peaceful.
Safe.

There's love here.
There's no yelling.
No bruises.

No fear.

We just are.

I breathe.
I let the moment hold me.

And when I open my eyes,
my face is soaked with tears.

But my body isn't shaking from fear this time.
It's shaking from release.

And to my right —
still in the room —
I feel it.
That boulder.

It's real.
It's there beside me.

I finally set it down.

I don't know if I'll pick it back up.
Maybe I'll leave it here.
Maybe I'll roll it somewhere else.
Maybe I'll carve it into something new.

I don't have to decide right now.

All I know
is that something changed in this session.

I think this is where healing
began.

It was raw.
It was painful.
It was beautiful.
It was
necessary.

I braved the storm again.

🌿 Closing Reflection

This session mattered more than I expected.
The professionalism of my therapist—
her steadiness,
her knowing,
her own healing—
played such a vital role.

She created enough light in all that darkness,
enough safety for me to meet my protector,
to see him,
to understand him,
and to honor him.

And that changed everything.

Because when we name it,
we can face it.
When we face it,
we can feel it.
And when we feel it,
we can begin.

❖A Question to Sit With
What would happen if you thanked the part of you
you've spent your whole life trying to destroy?

✧ ECHOES

The Calm After the Tempest

That day,
the session unfolded
in the quiet hours of midday.
On the drive home,
my mind was calm —
strangely still.
I stared through walls,
into the distance
of where I was headed:
home.

I was exhausted.
Awake.
Peaceful.
And shaken —
all at once.

This is what happens after EMDR.
Not always a crash of sobbing,
not always chaos.
Sometimes it's a quiet storm
that rains softly inside —
clouds hanging low,
yet something in you
finally still.

I went home.
Didn't sleep.
Just sat with myself.
No need to fix.
No urge to flee.
I held my kids closer.
My daughter tighter.
Hugged my wife deeper —
with more presence,

more truth.
My heart was open.
And no one needed me
to be anything else.

The afternoon passed
in quiet processing.
But that night —
the bad dreams came.
Rage broke through my sleep.
I tossed.
Turned.
Woke up drenched in it.
No rest.
No escape.

By morning,
I was wrecked —
tired
and raw.

The protector inside me
rose again.
Clenched fists.
Hot tears.
Confused.
Ready to fight.

But I didn't fight it.
Didn't judge it.
Didn't name it.
I just let it be.
The anger.
The grief.
The old reflex to brace.

And with every wave,
I met it with breath.
With love.
With stillness.

I calmed the protector.
Held him steady.
He was waking from an old dream,
still gripping his weapon.
Still ready for war.

But I reminded him —
he doesn't need to carry it anymore.
He doesn't need to pick up that rock.
We left the armor
in that room.
With my therapist.
It's not mine to wear now.

Not today.

All day,
I repeated that truth.
Whispered it
like a prayer
to the trembling parts of me.

And slowly,
something softened.
Something exhaled.

I found peace.
Not perfect.
Not complete.
But real.

I got ready
to return —
to walk back into the room,
to hold the paddles,
feel the buzzers,
and face the next wave.

But this time —
this time,
I'd go in
without my protector.

This is me now.

Chapter Seven

Into the Storm

EMDR Session
Rage, Sadness, and the Desire for Payback

I walk into my therapist's office
having a good day.
I'm joyful.
Happy.
I crack a few jokes.
We laugh.

What I love most about EMDR
is how we've found a way to laugh
in the face of trauma.

Laughter is healing.
To speak of something so vivid,
so violent,
so dark—
and still find a moment
to laugh.

Because sometimes,
even inside the worst memories,
something absurd
or oddly timed
breaks through.

And that rupture—
it opens something.
It makes room
for healing.

That day,
I was joyful.
As I can be

when I'm masking.

I smile.
I joke.
I perform.

But under it—
I'm raging.
I'm shaking.
I'm in fight or flight.

I got really, really good at masking,
and my therapist saw it.

She asks,
"When do you think you first learned to mask?"

I had to sit with that.
I think I started around 12.
At school.
Around family.
In public.

Mask on.
Smile set.
Don't let it show.

She hands me the buzzers.
They fit in my palms like memory.
Familiar.

I loosen my grip.
The soft pulsing begins—
left, right, left, right.

She doesn't push.
She just sits with me,
open, grounded, waiting.

And then—
I start to speak.

I'm in the storm.

Not inside it yet—
but watching it build.

The clouds darken.
The wind sharpens.
Lightning.
Gusts.

It's not a storm—
it's a hurricane.

Rage.
Sadness.
Grief.
All of it rising.

"What are you noticing right now?" she asks.

"I'm overwhelmed."

I'm furious.
Not at a memory.
Not at the little boy on the bench.
Not even the protector.

This is me now.

I'm enraged
that they did this to me.
That my life
has been built from pain.
That I was used.
Beaten.
Broken.

And I'm angry at myself.

For the way I sometimes erupt—
at home,
with friends,
with people I love.

Throwing things.

Yelling.
Scaring myself.
Scaring them.

This is trauma.
This is the aftershock.
This is fight or flight
in real time.

I don't remember
what it feels like to live
outside of this.

My nervous system is fried.
My body clenched.
My jaw locked.
I realize—
I'm gripping the buzzers too tight.

I hear them creak.
Plastic straining.

My hands are shaking.
I'm curled over.
And I'm crying.

I didn't even know I was crying.
But I'm speaking through it.

That's new.

Usually when I cry,
my voice disappears—
choked out by something old,
something scared.

But today,
I speak.

**She says gently,
"You're with a lot right now. Do you want to stay with it... or
check in with the body?"**

I nod.
I stay.

And what I want—
is to go back.

Not to comfort the little boy.
But to drag them
into this storm.

To make them see what they did.
To feel it.
To hurt.
Like I hurt.

But I don't want revenge.
Not really.

It won't fix it.
It won't make it stop hurting.

I realize—
the anger I'm holding
is still holding the trauma.

I can't forget it.
I'm not ready to forgive.
But maybe—
I can let go of this grip.

Even just a little.

I'm still raging.
Still grieving.

But then—
a flicker of stillness.
A question:

Can I accept this?

And if I do—
will it bring peace?

Will it lighten the weight?

So I try.

Just for a moment,
I try.

But it doesn't feel like peace.
It feels like floating in darkness.
Chaos all around.

I don't see my trauma.
I don't see my parents.
I don't even see the little boy.
Or the protector.
Or myself.

All I see
is the storm.

I'm inside it now.

Lightning,
wind,
screams,
shattered debris.

This is what my nervous system feels like.
This is my fight or flight—
made visible.

This session isn't about the past.
Not a memory.
Not a scene.

It's about now.
This feeling.
This vibration.

Then, in the stillness between sobs,
her voice comes through—gentle, steady:,
"Notice where you feel that in your body."

I do.
It's immediate.
My chest—tight, burning.
My arms—heavy.
My hands—buzzing, like I'm still gripping the storm itself.

It's strong.
Every part of me feels it.

I cry—
a different kind of crying.

Grief.
Sorrow.
The ache of never having felt safe.

I'm angry all the time.
Wired to protect.
Everyone.
Everything.

My life is upside down.

I want to blame them.
My parents.

They did this.
They brought the storm.
They activated my fight or flight.

But blame doesn't set me free.

I hear her voice, soft and even:
"You're here now. Just notice what's shifted."

My therapist gently guides me back—
to my safe place.

I go.
Exhausted.
Tears still falling.

I grieve.

Not them.
Not the memory.
Me.

I cry for myself.
The self I armored.
The self I silenced.
The self I never let feel.

It's confusing.
And comforting.
And terrifying.

But it's real.

And in that quiet place—
I just sit.

Listen.
Feel.
Be.

She says softly,
"Whenever you're ready... you can bring your attention back to the room."

I do.

And I'm calm.

Somehow.

After all that.
Calm.

My breathing steady.
My body still.

She holds eye contact—
steady,
kind,
safe.

She doesn't evaluate.

Doesn't judge.

She says,
"You stayed with a lot just now."

I speak.
Words spill out
with something like gratitude.

Raw.
Unfiltered.

Because as brutal as this is—
it's the only thing
that reaches me.

EMDR.

It cuts through the armor.
Shatters the silence.
Finds the locked rooms
and blows the doors off.

I face it all—
the broken pieces,
the ripped timelines,
the memories that nearly took me down.

And I don't have to hold them
alone.

This therapy—
it's not easy.
It's not clean.
But it works.

For the first time,
I feel like I'm in the healing—
not just surviving it.

I cry.
In front of someone
I barely know.

But I trust her.
With everything.

She's not just a canvas.

She's a guide.
She stays.

She doesn't run
when the storm rises.

🌿 Closing Reflection

In the storm—
in the middle of rage and sorrow—
I found something strange: a calm.

Not the kind that means it's over.
But a quiet center,
right in the eye.

Anger is loud.
But it is not all of me.

It's part of my story.
Not the whole one.

Healing is showing up to pain
without running.

Letting it come.
Letting it be.

Then slowly—
softly—
releasing it.

The storm still rages,
but I am not lost in it.

I'm learning
to be the stillness inside it.

Acceptance isn't forgetting.
It's carrying the weight
differently.

Not holding tight
to what keeps me clenched.

Not yet forgiving.
Not yet fixing.
Just being here.

Present.
Alive.
Healing.

I'm starting to trust myself again.

That I can weather this.
That I can find my way
through the storm.

This is not the end.
It's the beginning.

❖A Question to Sit With
What pain are you still holding?
What would happen if you let go—
even just a little—
today?

✧ ECHOES

The Gratitude that Held Me

After that session,
I went home.
Laid on the couch.

My wife knew.
She didn't ask.
She just let me rest.

Without thinking,
I dozed off.
Exhausted.

I slept —
deep, long —
four hours of stillness.

When I woke,
the house was quiet.
Peaceful.

I stood.
Looked around.
And felt it —

Gratitude.

Grateful I built this.
This safety.
This softness.

For my wife.
For my kids.

No trauma here.
No one walking on eggshells.

They can sleep.
They are protected.
They are free.

There's joy.
There's peace.
There's love.
Empathy.
Acceptance.

I cried.
Cried with gratitude.

Because I created this.
Something I never had.

How did I become a good man
after everything I survived?

How did I not break
into someone colder?
Crueler?
Gone?

Somehow —
somehow —
I ran to the light.

And that is why,
from this point forward,
I will shine.

Shine as bright as I can.
Because the brighter the light,
the less darkness remains.

Nothing hides in the light.

My trauma can't hide anymore —
because I'm shining on it.

Together —
with my therapist,

with EMDR,
with the storm —

we are the light now.

I'm starting to find myself again.

I still shake.
I still wonder —
will that ever go away?

Fight or flight still rages.
Still pulses through me.

But I am healing.
I am releasing.

It is working.
EMDR is saving me.

🌀 Chapter Eight

Sister Wounds

EMDR Session
Facing the Pain Between Us

I sit in the cozy chair
across from my therapist.
It's raining.
Of course it is.
The sky feels what I'm feeling.

Sad.
Confused.

I ask for the paddles—
the buzzers.
She hands them to me.
I go to my safe place.

And I'm already crying.
I don't even try to hold it in.
I don't try to leave
the place I built—
the place inside me.

I speak.
And eventually,
it fades.

Not like a storm.
Just…
fades.

This is a different kind of pain.
This trauma feels different.

I go back.

To the day I came home from school
and something was off.

There was a woman in the house—
from the church.
She greeted me
with my brother.

Then she said:
"Your sister is in the hospital."

I was in fifth grade.
It had been a beautiful day.
Sunny.
Fun.

But when I walked through that door,
the fear returned.
The anxiety.
The unnamed feelings
that lived in my body
with no explanation.

Where was my sister?
What happened?

My sister was born autistic.
But no one talked about it.
My parents hid it.

"She'll grow out of it," they said.
"She'll speak one day."

So I waited.
Waited for something to change.
Waited for a conversation.

But all I got was:
flapping.
screaming.
spinning.
crying.

staring—
through me.

And now,
a stranger from church
was the one to tell me
my sister had stopped breathing.

She'd had a seizure.
She was in the hospital.

I didn't know if she'd live.
I didn't know what death meant.
Not yet.

But I felt the shift.
The way silence moved in.
The way no one said anything.
The way the house grew colder.

I don't remember her coming home.

I just remember
when it happened again.

Months passed.
It was winter this time.

Dark.
Heavy.
Cold.

I was asleep.
My father was at work.
My brother—
I'm not sure.

He's always there in my memories,
except that night.

That night,
it was just me.

And then—

My mother's voice,
screaming.
"Help! Help!"

I ran down the hall,
bare feet on the wood floor.

And I saw them.

My sister—on the floor.
My mom—over her,
performing CPR.

Her lips were blue.
Her body, still.

A phone nearby.
911 already on the line.

The operator's voice
floated in the background—
distant,
muted.

Everything was happening so fast.
And yet,
it all felt slow.

I remember touching my sister's hand.
Cold.
Lifeless.

I remember rubbing my mother's back
as she cried.

It was the first time
she asked for my help.

Not to punish.
Not to yell.
But to save.

I was just a boy—
but I became a man in that moment.

At least,
that's what it felt like.

The shock
pulled me up from childhood
and dropped me into something
I didn't understand.

Then the paramedics arrived.
They rushed in,
checked her pulse,
took over.

And then they left.
With her.
And my mom.

The door stayed open.
The cold came in.

I was left alone.

I sat there.
Frozen.
Shaking.
Numb.

Did she make it?
Was she gone?
What had just happened?

I prayed.
Even though I didn't know how.

I prayed
the way a scared child does—
with broken words
and a trembling voice.

Eventually,

I crawled into my bed.
I cried myself to sleep.

When I woke, it was still dark.

But my dad and brother were home.

Dad said she was alive.
In the hospital.
Breathing.

And then he left again.

I stayed.
With my brother.

But I don't remember
anything after that.

That's where the memory ends.
That's where I froze.

But it wasn't the last time.

There was another.

We had moved.
Lived with my grandparents then.

A fresh start, they said.

I thought maybe things would change.
Maybe someone would protect me.
Maybe now the beatings would stop.
Maybe the yelling would quiet.

But it didn't.

The abuse just got more creative.
More secretive.
More controlled.

And then—
one day.

I was in my room
with my sister.

Music played.
She was laughing.
Flapping.
Giggling.

We were… connected.

In a way
I hadn't felt before.

And then she stopped.

No laughter.
No movement.
Just a stare—
through me.

Drool spilled from her mouth.
Her lips turned blue.
She collapsed.

I picked her up.
Ran with her in my arms—
into the kitchen,
screaming for my mom.

"She's not breathing!"

Panic.

My mom dropped everything,
started CPR.

I grabbed the phone.
Tried to dial.
911.

But my hands weren't working.
I pressed too many numbers.
Panicked.

Dropped the phone.
Ran outside.

I don't even know why I ran.
Instinct, maybe.

I just needed help.

And then,
there he was—
a man working on the water system.

I pulled him into the house.
He called 911.

By the time they arrived,
my mom had brought her back.

She was breathing.
Barely.
But breathing.

And then,
once again—
they left.

And I was alone.

Again.

No one came back for a while.
The house was too quiet.
The music still played in my room.

But I turned it off.
And cried.

No one told me it wasn't my fault.
No one said,
"You did the best you could."

No one said anything.

So I blamed myself.

Again.

I carried that weight for years.

That somehow,
I broke her.

Because I was so bad when my mom was pregnant with her —
always getting yelled at,
always making things harder —
that's what they told me.

That somehow,
I failed her.

And I never said any of it—
not out loud—
until that day
in the therapist's chair.

I had the buzzers in my palms.
My legs felt tense.
My breath—shallow.
My chest—tight.

Then I heard my therapist.

Her voice anchored me—
gentle,
present,
real.

"Go to your safe place.
When you're ready—
you can open your eyes."

So I did.

Slowly.

Back in the room.
Back in the now.

Still trembling,

but whole.

Still healing,
but here.

🌿 Closing Reflection

This session taught me something I didn't expect—
that blame can sneak in quietly,
camouflaged as responsibility.

I had been holding the guilt
like it was mine to bear.

I believed their words,
even long after they stopped saying them out loud.

Because guilt that deep
doesn't need to be spoken.

It lives in the silence.
It grows in the spaces
where no one says the truth.

But this time—
I said it.

I let the tears fall.
I saw her face.

I remembered the blue lips,
the sound of my mother screaming,
the cold room.

And I didn't run.
I didn't freeze.

I breathed through it.

That's what healing looks like sometimes.

Not clarity.
Not closure.

Just enough air
to survive the memory.

Just enough space
to hold the pain with two hands—
and not be consumed by it.

❖A Question to Sit With
Who did you once believe you had to become
in order to protect someone you loved—
and are you still holding that role,
even now?

✧ ECHOES

Healing the Wounds Between Us

When I came home
after that session,
I sat at the table with my wife.
My body still buzzing.
My chest sore, like I'd cried underwater.

I spoke out loud—
words still raw,
still fragile.

She's known me through it all.
She knows my sister.
Knows the weight I carry.

She said,
"It wasn't your fault."

I nodded—
because some part of me already knew.
But hearing it out loud
felt like a lifeline
thrown across the dark.

She reminded me,
**"Your sister had you with her.
You stayed.
You gave her safety
in the only ways you knew how."**

And in that moment,
the guilt came back—
sharp, fierce, alive.
That *I left her behind feeling*.
That ache.

I escaped.
She didn't.
She stayed with the ones who broke us.

I told myself—
Maybe this is a thread for another session.
Something to unravel slowly,
safely.
Not today.

Today,
I just needed space to be.
To let it settle.
To hold the weight
without trying to carry it.

Because in EMDR,
healing doesn't come from rushing.
It comes in the quiet after—
when your body softens,
and your mind
finally begins
to let go.

I cried.

And as the tears came,
something loosened.
The blame
that had clung to my ribs
began to slip.

Like dark ink
spilling into water.

It didn't vanish.
But it faded.
Just enough
to make room
for something else—

Hope.
Compassion.
A small seed of peace.

And maybe that's how healing begins.

Not with answers.
Not with resolution.
But with breath.
With tears.
With letting go—
one moment
at a time.

Chapter Nine
The Attack That Shattered Us

This chapter reflects a traumatic event that led to later
EMDR processing.
When Violence Reached My Daughter

I was already in counseling
for my trauma—
but EMDR hadn't started yet.

Only a few sessions in
when something happened—
not in memory,
but right there
in real time.

Up until that day,
I still spoke to my parents.
I was working through the trauma they caused,
and somehow,
still seeking connection.

Two days
after Christmas.

We'd planned for them to come by—
to exchange gifts
with my youngest daughter.
She was eleven.

This chapter
has no buzzers.
No quiet office.
No place to close my eyes
and go inward.

This is trauma,

live.

The first time
it wasn't just me.
The first time
my daughter stood beside me
when the storm broke loose.

The phone rings.
It's them.
They're running late.

We're tight on time.
So I say gently,
"If it's too late,
we can reschedule."

The yelling starts.
Cussing.

Something hot
rises in me.

I hold it
as long as I can—
then snap.

"I just need you
to get it together."

They hang up.

I call back.
"Please don't hang up.
You always do this."

Now I'm yelling.
They're blaming.

I become
the protector again—
fighting back.

They hang up.

I look at my daughter.
Still waiting.
Still hopeful.

She's excited.
Smiling.

I step into my office,
call my wife.

"They're not coming," I say.
"They're mad again."

Then—

my daughter runs in.
"They're here!"
Beaming.
Jumping.

I sigh.
"I guess we're doing this."

I go to the door.

I see my mom
in the driveway—
tossing gifts into the snow.
Screaming.
The wind catching the paper
as it flies.

"What are you doing?" I shout.

But before the words finish—

She charges.

The door slams open,
cracks the frame.

She grabs me by the throat.

Hits my chest.
My face.

Everything stills.

I freeze.

I'm not 42.

I'm seven.
Or five.
Or nine.

Small.
Voiceless.
Trapped in a moment
that stretches
and never ends.

Terror coils inside me.

I want to cry.
To scream.
To run.

But—

a fire ignites.

The protector returns.
Teeth grit.
Fists clench.

I look at her—
and say,
"I'm 42 years old.

You don't get to do this anymore.
You don't have that power."

I rip her hand off my throat.

I'm seconds from swinging—

when I catch movement.

My daughter.

Standing frozen.

Clutching the stuffed animal
I gave her—
the same one I held
when I was her age,
watching my father
fight his father
in the kitchen.

Time splits.

I see myself
in her eyes.

And I stop.

I freeze.

I push my mom back.

Out the door.

She's screaming—
rage uncontainable.

She's dangerous when wild.
Anything nearby
can become a weapon.

The coats.
The shoes.
The mirror.

I brace.

But I am lion now.
Armored in pain.
And fire.

I push her out.
Slam the door.
Lock it.

"Get out!" I scream.

She hurls curse words.
My father joins in,
banging on the glass—
"Your dad did this!"
"You'll never see us again!"
"He's to blame!"

They aim their venom
at my daughter—
try to make her doubt me.
Blame me.

I beg.
I plead—
not for myself,
but to protect her.

"Let's do the gifts.
It's okay.
Please."

But they don't hear me.
Only rage.

My mom lunges again—
I kick her back.

My dad explodes—
"You're the reason
we were homeless!
You're the reason
your sister is autistic!
You're the reason
everything went wrong!"

The words bounce off me.

I'm shaking.
Soaked in sweat.
Heart pounding.

They leave.

Silence.
The door
locks behind them.

I am wrecked.

My daughter is shaking—
staring out the window
at gifts in the snow.

Joy
ripped open.

I lift her up,
hold her tight.

"I'm sorry," I whisper.
"This isn't your fault.
It's not mine either.
They're just like this."

She pulls back—
eyes wide,
voice cracking—

"Why would anyone
want to hurt you, Dad?

Why would they do that
to their own son?

Don't they love you?"

I don't have an answer.

Only tears.

I say,

"If you ever have questions,
I'm here.
Always."

We sit.
Wrapped in silence.
On the couch.

For an hour.

Holding each other.

And in that hour—

I make a decision.

It's over.

No more chances.

No more doorways
left unlocked.

I remember the promise
I made
the day she was born—

"I will never let anyone
hurt you.
I will fight
to protect you."

But I let them in.

And they hurt her.

Just like they hurt me.

But this time—
I saw it.

I didn't look away.

And I ended it.

Because if not that day—
then the next.
And next time
could be worse.

🌿 Closing Reflection

Trauma doesn't always come
dressed as memory.

Sometimes,
it kicks down the door—
while your child is watching.

That day,
the lines between past and present
blurred.

I had to face the truth:
Some people never change.
Some wounds don't soften
just because we want them to.

But in that rupture,
I found my power—
not as a victim,
but as a protector.

I chose my daughter's safety
over ties to the past.

That choice broke something open—
but it also set us free.

Healing is not tidy.
It's raw.
Messy.
Painful.

But sometimes,
the fiercest kind of love
is choosing to shut the door
on what harms you—
so that what you love most

can finally
breathe.

❖A Question to Sit With
What boundaries do you need to set
to protect your peace—
and the peace of those you love—
even when it means saying goodbye
to people
you once hoped would change?

✧ ECHOES

The Day I Didn't Become What Hurt Me

This isn't an EMDR hangover.
It's not about the hours after a session.

It's truth.
Raw.
The kind that settles in your bones
after years of surviving
what should've broken you.

I'm here
because I fought to be.

I've faced every demon,
every dragon,
every moment that tried to end me.
And I stayed.

Not because it was easy.
But because I knew
somewhere deep —
I was worth being here.

And now I know:
my purpose is this.
To take what I lived through
and place it, gently,
into someone else's shaking hands —
someone still in it.

That day…
I could've become what hurt me.

The rage was there.
The destruction.
The old fire that would've burned it all down —
my safety,

my peace,
everything my wife and I fought to build.

And I wanted to.
For days,
for weeks,
I kept replaying it.

All the ways I could've stopped it.
Fought louder.
Fought meaner.
Fought like I used to.

But my daughter…
She was standing there.

And the lion stayed still.

Because if I let go —
if I roared like the wounded child inside me wanted to —
I wouldn't just be fighting them.
I'd be shattering her safety.

She didn't need my rage.
She needed me whole.

That moment…
it felt like time stopped.
But trauma doesn't move in straight lines.

My brain was a split-screen.
Past, present, and future
all bleeding together.

The protector.
The child.
The father.
All of me —
at war.

And somehow,
stillness won.

I held it.
I walked away.

Not because I was weak.
But because I knew:
she didn't need to carry my scars.

Toxic people will do anything
to drag you back into the storm.
To bait you.
To steal your peace.

My parents had chances.
They had time.
But they stayed radioactive.

I chose light.
I chose distance.
I chose to run
as far from what they were
as I could.

Until I couldn't.
Until I froze.
Until I couldn't outrun the flashbacks anymore.

That's when my wife saw it.
That I was drowning inside.

And that's when I found two people
who didn't flinch.

Fay.
Shirley.

They didn't heal me.
They made space
for me to heal.

They handed me the buzzers —
those small, buzzing lifelines —
and stayed with me
as I walked back into the fire.

And I didn't get lost.

Because they stayed.
And so did I.

Even when the memories bled out.
Even when the demons came close.
They didn't turn away.

They held steady.
And I held on.

And that's how I lived.
That's how I didn't become
what hurt me.

⊚ Chapter Ten
The Night I Held the Weight of Their War

EMDR Session
Caught Between Chaos and Survival

I got to my therapist's a little early.
Sitting in the waiting room, thinking about
what I was going to find in the storm today.

Where are we going to go?
How deep are we going to go? How intense?
What might I find?
What door am I going to open?
How exhausted will I be afterward?

Not looking forward to tomorrow
and the rage that might come from this session.
But I know I need this.
We've been working hard.
I'm committed.

I hear the door open.
She says hi, motions me in—her voice comforting, her tone
pleasant.
Her room inviting.

All the nerves go away.

I move forward, find my spot, sit in my comfy chair.
She sits across from me and asks,
"How are you doing today? Where would you like to start?"

I tell her I'm not quite sure,
but I can feel the paddles—the buzzers—
as soon as I hold them, they'll guide me.

She asks,

"Do you want to go to your safe place, or go right into the session?"

I choose my safe place.
I grab the buzzers.
As they begin to vibrate, I settle in.
I'm very familiar with this now.
Relaxed. I'm there.
In my safe place. Breathing.
Calm. Collected.
Imagining summertime.

I spend a few minutes there, then let her know—I'm ready.
Ready to go wherever it might be.

The buzzers change pattern.
The moment they do,
I fall face first into the storm.

Memories come crashing—
painful, disturbing, dark—
ripping apart the fabric of my innocence,
of all I thought life was at that time.

It felt so real in the moment.
I remember.

We were in a new house.
I was 15.
My brother had moved out.
Just me, my sister, and my parents.

New school.
New life.

It had been a while since the last beating,
the last mental abuse,
since chaos ripped through my world.

Not long enough.

Quickly, I remembered that night.
I went upstairs to my bedroom,

went to sleep—eager, looking forward to school.

I still didn't enjoy my home life.
I was at a pivotal time—
learning new things, testing freedom.
Curfews loosening.
Living a bit wild,
because I didn't know what life should be.

No structure. No boundaries. No direction.
I was still running.
Running from what might happen.
Fight or flight had its full grip on me—
I just didn't know it yet.
But I felt it.

As I slept,
I heard my mom's voice scream,
"Help!"
Yelling for me.

I jumped out of bed, ran downstairs.
In my mind, all I think about—
this same cry has always meant one thing—
my sister is having a seizure.

Is this the last time I see her?
I brace myself.

I reach the stairs.
But when I round the corner into the living room—
I see my parents fighting.

My sister isn't there.
She's not on the floor.
She's not part of this scene.
This has nothing to do with her.

Before I can react—
I'm pulled into their fight.
Grabbing. Pulling. Yelling.

Then I see the gun.

My mom has the gun.
My dad's hands are around hers, holding it.
He's yelling,
"She's trying to kill herself. We've got to get the gun away."

I step between them, reach in—
too many hands on the gun.
Too much resistance.
Fighting. Chaos. Screaming.

I back away. Try again.
I find a moment.
I pry the gun from my mom's hands
and hand it to my dad.

Then, as I turn—
my dad puts the gun to his head.

I fight with him.
Knock the gun from his hand.
Push him to the floor.
Grab the gun.
Back up, holding it—
motioning both of them to sit on the couch.

I'm scared. Shaking.
But I hold the power.

They look at me, confused.
They follow my order.
They sit.

I sit across from them, holding the gun,
not knowing what to do.

I ask,
"What is going on? Why is this happening?
You have to stop. I can't take this anymore."

My therapist says softly,
"Just notice that."

Now we're addressing the trauma.
Bringing it up.
I'm nervous. Afraid.

They look at me.
We mirror the same energy—
anger, hate, sadness, chaos, trauma.

My mom is silent.
My dad speaks.

"Your mother had an affair. She cheated on me.
I don't know what to do.
Should I take her back? Should we kick her out? Should we let her
stay?"

He calls her names—slut, whore, cheater.

His betrayal burns me.

I'm upset. Worn out. Lost. Hurt.
This isn't a shock.
Her affair doesn't hit as hard as it could.

All I see are these two people—
my parents—putting me through hell again.
Traumatizing me.
Pulling me into their chaos.
Making me make decisions.
Forcing me to be a man.
To grow up.
To carry their pain.

I sit there, holding the gun,
pointing it at the floor,
not knowing what to do.

My brother walks in.
It's late—about 2 a.m.
He and two friends.

They see me with the gun.
They laugh. Joke.

Say I'm crazy.

My brother grabs the gun, walks it to the bookshelf, sets it down.
Pulls the bullets out.
Throws them in a drawer.
Walks out with his friends—
like nothing is wrong.
Like this is normal.

He didn't experience the trauma like I did.
He moved out.
Spent time with a girlfriend.
Escaped.

I feel like he left me in it.
Maybe he didn't know.
Maybe he did.

This was normal.
To him. To us.

Our family.
Our friends.
They didn't see it. Didn't get it.

His friends didn't understand.

These things made me feel like this was normal.

My sister never woke from the chaos.
She didn't see this.
I was thankful for that.

But it was so late.
I dragged myself to bed.
Tired.

Why is this happening?

I got up for school.
Exhausted.
Teachers thought I was on drugs.
Sleepy. Distracted.

They didn't know.
I couldn't tell them.

My parents warned me—
if I say anything, Child Services would take my sister.
I'd be ripped from this home.

It didn't sound so bad.
But they made it seem like it would end everything I ever had or wanted.

For some reason—
I don't know why—
I held on to this.
This environment.
These people.
Who hurt me.
Who abused me.

I'm saying this out loud.
I sense the room.
I'm still in the therapy chair.
Still holding the buzzers.

I get jolted back.
But the memories are fresh.
The feelings, there.

I didn't realize I was crying.
Sobbing.
Breathing hard.

My therapist speaks,
"What are you feeling?"

"Angry. Upset. Why?
Why did this happen?
Why do I still hold this?"

"It was so long ago."

I break down.
Can't stop crying.

Can't catch a breath.

My therapist holds space.
Lets the room be peaceful.
It's quiet.

I hear the buzzers—
left, right, speeding up, slowing down.
Shifting me.
Helping me move trauma.

She says gently,
"What comes up now?"

I go back into the storm—harder.
More memories flash—
fast as light.

A projector in my mind—
showing everything.
Fragments. Pieces.
Things that don't belong.

Because I shouldn't be traumatized.
But I am.
And I've lived this.

I'm so sad.
So scared.

I remember when my mom cheated.

Trauma is out of order in my brain.
You'd think I'd recall it in sequence.
But memories twist.
They scatter.

How do we clean this up?
Collect it?

My therapist says,
"Keep going. You're doing good."

I take a breath.
Fear. Anxiety.
The shakes hit.

Fight or flight—fully activated.
Squeezing buzzers.
Clenching teeth.
Jaw tight.
Arms tense.

The protector shows up.
The beast.
The lion.

My armor comes back.

I recall another moment.

Before school.
All of us in the van.
My dad drives my mom to the airport.
She was going to see the person she had an affair with.

My dad must have known.

When we got home, I went to get ready for school.
Walked past the garage.
I saw it.

A noose.
A ladder.
A rope.

Was it deliberate?
Was I supposed to see this?
Was I supposed to stop him?

I ran in.
Climbed the ladder.
Took it down.
Kicked the ladder away.

Yelled,

"What are you doing?"

He said nothing.
Cried.
Told me to leave.
Yelled. Called me names.
Said it was my fault.

"Get out."

I didn't go to the bus stop.
I ran upstairs.
My sister wasn't safe.
I stayed home.
Skipped school.

I was so upset.
Why did they want to die?
Why did I care?

They abused me.
Beat me.
But I knew nothing else.

No place to turn.
No place to go.

Why?

I start to cry.
I'm angry.

I want to take that rage out.
On the bullies.
The teachers.
Anybody who challenged me.

Because no one hurt me more than my parents already did.

I thought I was fearless.
The lion in armor.

But now—

after all these sessions—
after going into the storm—
I realize…

I had more fear and anxiety in that armor
than I do now.

Healing brings peace.
Tames the beast.
Calms the lion.

EMDR changes me.
Reshapes me.
Unlocks doors.

The memory moves—
but the pain isn't as strong.
Some still need time.

I pause.
A couple minutes.
Free falling.
Floating.
Fading.

Tears stop.
Calm.
Worn out.

My therapist says,
"Let's go back to your safe place.
Take deep breaths.
When you're ready, open your eyes."

I don't want to stay too long.
Five deep breaths.
Grounded.
Ready.

I open my eyes.
Hard to make eye contact.

Not ashamed. Not afraid.

Just closed off.
Wanting to hide in the smallest corner.

But her gaze—
her empathy, her presence—
her stillness—

She softens me.
Grounds me.
Shows me I'm safe.

Without speaking.
Just her body language.
Her attention.

We finished our session.
I thanked her.

🌿 Closing Reflection

If you've carried pain like this,
if you've ever held more than your share—
I want to speak directly to you.

This chapter was one of the hardest to write.
To relive.
To survive.

But EMDR gave me the courage to enter it.
To stay in the storm
instead of running.

My therapist didn't fix it.
She didn't rescue me.
She witnessed.
Held space.

And sometimes, that's everything.

I'm learning now that healing
isn't about forgetting—
it's about remembering differently.
Carrying the story with less weight.

If this resonates with you,
my hope is that you'll find
your own safe place,
your own rhythm of healing.

You don't have to hold it all forever.

❖A Question to Sit With
When did you first feel responsible
for someone else's pain?
Was it ever truly yours to carry?

And if you could set that weight down—
just for a moment—
what might your hands be free to hold instead?

✧ ECHOES

This Is What After Feels Like

After the session,
my wife greeted me at the door.
She hugged me.
I needed it.

I hugged her back.
She knows the story.
She knows my parents—
too well.

She asked,
"How was your session?"

I said,
"It was rough."

Then I broke.
Just—
broke.

I don't usually cry in front of her.
But I did.
Because it was too much.

Not grief exactly—
fear.
It scared me.
To go back there.
To feel it again.

We held each other.
I kept crying.

Later that night,
I got angry.
Then numb.
Then cried again.

At some point, I walked into my daughter's room.
She was asleep.

I sat on the edge of her bed,
rubbed her back gently.
Watched her breathe.

And I cried.
Again.

"I'm so glad you never had to go through this,"
I whispered.
"I'm so glad you're safe."

I cried because
I made that safety.
I cried because
I never had it.

I cried because
there was a time I wasn't okay.
Not even close.

Before the counselors.
Before EMDR.

And I cried because—
what if I had passed it on?
What if she ever felt
what I used to feel?

But I was trying.
Even when the trauma leaked out.
Even when I didn't know how to stop it.

I cried because
this work is finally reaching places
I thought were already dead.

I cried because
there's still hope.

The next day,
I couldn't feel much.
Just tired.
Hollowed out.

I didn't want to go back.
Didn't want to do another round of this.

Every session cracks something open.
And I come home
wrecked.
Raging.
Confused.
Gone.

But over time—
that feeling softens.

It shifts into
"I need to go back."
"This is working."
"I feel different."

You can't shortcut this.
You have to walk through the wreckage.
You have to sit in the pain.

And if this is what healing looks like—
I'll keep going.

Not just for me.
But for the people I love.

For the person
I'm still trying to become.

This is what after looks like.
Not clean.
Not fixed.
But honest.

If you're here too—
if you're in the spiral—
I hope you come back.

EMDR cracked me open.
My counselor and my therapist held the space.

But I had to show up.

Healing didn't happen to me.
I met it halfway.

And that
made all the difference.

⊚ Chapter Eleven

Loss in the Bloodline

EMDR Session
Mourning My Cousin

I wasn't feeling any type of way that day.
I told my therapist,
"I'm okay.
Work is good.
I'm here."

I cracked a few jokes.
We laughed.
And then—
she asked,

"What would you like to focus on today?"

I pulled out my phone.
Opened my notes.

We'd been deep in EMDR for a while now—
deep enough that I'd started writing things down:
pain I couldn't ignore,
moments I didn't want to forget to process.

I made a list.
A long one.

That day,
I picked my cousin.

I lost him.
A few years ago.
He took his own life.

She handed me the buzzers.

Time to go into the storm.

I closed my eyes.
Let go.
Buzzers begin.
Left. Right. Left. Right.

I remember the phone call.

We had just moved to South Florida—
my wife, our girls,
chasing a new beginning.

It wasn't working out.
We were already planning to move back.
It was a turbulent time.

But we were together.
Still trying.

Then my phone rang.
It was my brother.
His voice:

"Blake killed himself."

My cousin.
Blake.

I froze.
Numb.
Disbelief.

Across the room,
my wife was watching TV.
She saw my face.

"What's wrong?" she asked.
"What happened?"

I couldn't speak.
My brother hung up.

This can't be real.

I was just about to call him—
invite him to visit.
Spend time.
Catch up.

I'd missed a few calls from him.
No voicemail.
No texts.

Now he was gone.

I broke down.
Heavy sobs.
Sudden, aching grief.

How?
Why?

He was beautiful.
Alive.
Light.

We talked all the time.
We had plans.
Big dreams.
Take over the world.
Start something of our own.

As kids, we didn't get much time together.
Our parents fought.
Kept us apart.

But when we were together—
it was everything.

He was pure energy.
Joy.
Wild and inspiring.

He served our country.
Did missions overseas.

He never told me much.
Said he wanted to protect me
from what he saw.

I never pushed.
Just told him I was here.

He never seemed depressed.
Never showed it.
No warning signs.
No darkness that I could see.

Just laughter.
Love.
Hustle.
Hope.

But now—
looking back—
I see the clues.

His Instagram posts.
Not cries for help—
but intensity.
Extreme moments.

Mountaintops.
Marathons.
Breaking records.
Doing everything full-out.
Living like there was no time to waste.

And then he was gone.

I said it out loud,
there in the safety of that room:

"I could've saved him.
If I'd just picked up.
If I'd called back."

My therapist's voice was soft, grounded:
"It's not your fault."

Gentle.
Clear.

"He may not have been calling for help.
Maybe he just wanted to hear your voice.
To feel connected
one more time.

None of it—
would have changed the outcome."

She paused. Then:
"The brain of someone who dies by suicide —
it actually looks different.
It's not thinking clearly.
It's overwhelmed, in survival mode."

And she was right.

I couldn't have changed it.

But what do I do with this weight?

I never grieved him.
Didn't go to the funeral.

We were in the middle of moving back.
Everything was chaos.
Timing was impossible.

My cousins were angry.
They didn't understand.

There were fights.
Conspiracies.
Rage in the texts.
Finger-pointing in every direction.

And I just sat there—
staring at my phone.
Silent.
Stunned.

How is he gone?
How is this real?

We were supposed to take over the world.

I didn't think this was trauma.

Not like the beatings.
Not like the gun.
Not like my sister turning blue.

But it is.
This is trauma too.

Loss that couldn't be stopped.
Grief that never got space.

I was grieving.
But didn't know how.

And just like that—
I was in my safe place.

The trees.
The river.
The quiet.

I saw his face again.
His laugh.
The ridiculous things he used to say.

I told my therapist stories.
The real ones.

We laughed.
I cried.
Then laughed again.

I didn't think you could do both at once.
But you can.
And I did.

It felt like something released.
Something unburied.
Something real.

We talked about Blake—
not about how he died,
but how he lived.

Who he was.
What he gave.

And for a moment—
it was beautiful.

🌿 Closing Reflection

This session helped me name a part of my trauma
I didn't even know counted.

Losing my cousin—
someone I loved deeply—
someone I never imagined would take his life—
hit me harder than I allowed myself to admit.

I didn't grieve when it happened.
I didn't make it to the funeral.

Life was in motion.
We were relocating.
I told myself I was too busy.
But the truth is—
I didn't know how to grieve.
Not for him.
Not then.

For years, all I felt was guilt.
Shame.
The constant what ifs.

What if I'd picked up?
What if I'd said more?

But this time—
in that quiet, safe room—
I heard something I hadn't felt before.

When my therapist said,
"It's not your fault,"
I didn't just hear the words.

I felt them.

I believed them.

And something in me softened.

She helped me understand that grief isn't always about what we've lost
—
sometimes it's about remembering what mattered
while they were still here.

I laughed through tears,
telling stories about Blake.

Not just grieving his absence—
but holding the presence
of who he was.

That laugh-cry moment?
It surprised me.
But it released something I'd carried in silence for too long.

And that—
that felt like healing.

❖A Question to Sit With
What if grief isn't something
we're meant to conquer or complete—
but something we learn to carry
with more compassion,
more memory,
and less guilt?

What if it's not about what we didn't do,
but about how we choose to remember
those we've lost—
and how we let their memory shape
the way we keep living?

✧ ECHOES
What Remains

That night, I went home and tried
to hold it together.

We sat at the dinner table—
my wife, my daughter,
me barely there.

I had to excuse myself.

The grief came fast.
Memories of my cousin—
his laugh, his face, the way we used to be.
I miss him.
God, I miss him.

I sobbed for hours.
Not an EMDR hangover.
Not trauma.
Loss.

Like it just happened.
Like I had just heard the news all over again.

My brain raced.
But not in panic—
in mourning.

So I went looking.

I found old photos.
Old videos—us laughing, messing around.
I wrote some things about him.
I put it all together
and emailed it to my therapist.

Not for insight.
Not for help.

Just to share him.
So she could see
how beautiful he was—
as a person,
as a soul.

How funny.
How full of life.

And it felt good.
To send that.
To give him that space.

She said he seemed funny.
A beautiful person.
Said he would've been cool to meet.

That meant something.

To hear someone else
say what I've been screaming inside.

EMDR is reshaping me.
Healing me.

And I can't deny it.
I accept it.

I'm grateful.

Not just for the work—
but for the chance.
The chance to be witnessed,
to grieve,
to need.

I thought I could save myself.
But now I see
how much help I really needed.

And I'm thankful
I finally let it in.

⊚ Chapter Twelve
Thrown: What the Body Remembers When Safety Is Gone

EMDR Session
The moment she lost control, and I lost my voice

This particular session started with tears.
I walked into the room already emotional.
I sat down in the comfy chair across from my therapist.
I asked for the paddles—the buzzers.
She handed them to me and gently asked,
"Where would you like to begin today?"

I felt like I was already in the storm before I even closed my eyes.
I couldn't get to my safe place.
We paused briefly—
just enough for me to breathe,
ground myself,
settle my body.

Then the buzzers began.
Left. Right. Left. Right.
The vibration took me straight into the heat—
into the memory,
into the trauma,
into the place where the pain lives.

I'm recalling a time when my brother was on the kitchen phone
with a friend.
I was goofing off—
swinging my arms in front of him.
My mom was doing dishes nearby.
My hand clipped the edge of the telephone cord,
ripping it from the wall.
The receiver dropped to the floor.
The cord hung, disconnected.

It was the house phone—
a replica of an old-fashioned wall unit
with "Thomas" engraved on a little plaque.
My parents loved that phone.
Praised it, even.

My brother screamed,
"What did you just do?!"

Before I could respond—
before I could explain—
my mom went from dishes
to full eruption.

She ran to me, grabbed my arm,
and threw me to the floor.

My brother bolted from the kitchen.
She ripped the phone from the wall—
jerking until wires snapped,
screws popped,
drywall tore.
Then she hurled the entire thing
through the back kitchen window.

Glass exploded—
everywhere.
All over the floor.
All over me.

I was frozen in shock. Crying.
In the therapy room, I was shaking.
My hands trembled as I held the paddles.

My therapist's voice came gently through the fog:
"What do you notice now?"

Before I could speak,
I was sobbing.
"I'm sorry," I said.
Over and over.
Through the tears, the fear, the pain.

"I'm sorry."

She turned to me then, in that memory—
grabbed me by both arms,
slammed me against the refrigerator,
screamed into my face:
"You did this. You're so bad."

And that's when I realized—
I was peeing.
Not just a little.
My body let go.
Terror flooded through every cell.

She noticed.
And she was still holding me—
gripping my armpits, my chest, my arms,
so tightly I couldn't breathe.
I thought she might crush me.

Then—
she pulled me away from the fridge,
dragged me through the air,
and hurled me down the basement stairs.

I hit the wall,
skipped the top half of the staircase,
slammed down the bottom third,
and landed face-first on the cement floor.

Silence.
Then a thought:
I'm out of her grip.
I made it.
I'm okay. I survived.

But I wasn't okay.
Not yet.

Above me, I heard rattling—
shuffling in the kitchen.

Then a drawer.
Silverware—knives, forks, spoons—
flying down the steps.
Metal clanging, bouncing, cutting, bruising.

A knife grazed my leg.
A fork jabbed my side.
Spoons hit my face.

Then came the toaster.
Its cord flailed behind it
like a tail of fury.
It slammed into the wall, cracked the drywall,
bounced down the stairs,
and hit me in the head.

I was lying there—
still, stunned,
bruised, bleeding,
in a tornado of destruction.

Object after object
crashed around me.
Some hit. Some missed.
But all of them were aimed at me.

Eventually, it stopped.

Silence again.
The air still.
No more glass.
No more metal.
Just the cold basement and my heartbeat.

I stayed there for a long time.
Shaking.
Bleeding.
Covered in urine.
Trying to clean up the mess.
Trying to clean up me.

But it was too much.

After about 20 minutes, I crept up the stairs.
At the top, I saw her—
my mom—collapsed on the floor.
Unconscious.

"Mom! Are you okay?" I cried.

She had high blood pressure.
Whenever she raged like this,
she would faint.
Collapse.

I ran to the back bedroom to get my brother.
He was hiding in bed, crying.
We both pulled her upright,
got her ice and water.
She came to slowly.
Then got up, walked to her room,
and went to sleep.

Not a word.

Me and my brother sat in silence,
waiting.
Wondering.
"What will Dad do when he gets home?"

We already knew.
He'd blame us.
Punish us.

And he did.
We were already in bed when we heard him.
"Boys!"
His voice thundered down the hallway.

The bedroom door burst open.
Light flooded in.

Panic.

He grabbed me by the leg—
dragged me from bed—

and started beating me with a wooden paddle.

Everywhere.
Front. Back.
Yelling. Blaming.
Five minutes, maybe more.

Then he tossed me into the room
and pulled my brother out.

I didn't hear screaming.
Just muffled voices.
Discipline. Control.
But not the sound of pain.
Not like mine.

My brother came back in,
crawled into bed,
and went to sleep.

I cried myself to sleep.

In the therapy room, I was crying again.
Shaking.

I whispered,
"How could someone do that to their kid?"

My therapist's voice came through:
"Just notice that."

I kept asking:
Why would they do this to me?
Was I not loved?
What did I do so wrong?

The phone wasn't even broken.
It could've just been plugged back in.

I was speaking,
but every word felt strangled.
Like the trauma was wrapped around my vocal cords.
Like it didn't want me to speak at all.

My throat hurt.
I could barely swallow.
I could barely breathe.

I cried harder.
Thought of all the times before this one—
all the other beatings,
the other moments of fear.

There were good days.
But the bad ones always seemed louder.
The lines between blurred.
Even the good days ended in pain.

I couldn't remember
what "normal" felt like.
I didn't feel loved.
I felt blamed.
Like I was the target.

In the therapy room, I went numb.
Anger, sadness, confusion—
 it was all tangled.

And then I went to my safe place.
Eyes still closed.
Buzzers still humming.

The trees surrounded me.
The river flowed.
Warmth. Sunlight.
Peace.

It felt like what I used to do as a kid—
sit in the backyard,
on the porch,
or run into the woods
after a beating.

I was grounding myself,
even then—
without knowing the word for it.

This safe place is real now.
A physical location.
One I visit often.
As an adult.

In this session,
it became an anchor.
A life raft.

I took a deep breath.
Opened my eyes.

"Wow," I said. "That was intense."

My therapist nodded.
"You stayed with it. That was important."

I nodded back,
so deeply grateful—
for her,
for EMDR,
for this room,
for going back into the storm
and making it out.

🌿 Closing Reflection

This session meant everything to me.
This memory had always been there—
sharp, alive, too loud to ignore.
It shaped me.
Scarred me.
Haunted me.

I didn't need EMDR to remember it—
I needed EMDR to survive it.

To feel it.
Release it.
Observe it without being devoured by it.

Now, it feels different.
Still there.
But not so sharp.
Not so loaded.

I'm not stuck anymore.
Not frozen.
Not enraged.

I'm not bleeding when I speak about it.
I'm not holding it like a secret weapon
against myself.

It still hurts—
but it doesn't control me.

And that feels like healing.

❖A Question to Sit With
What parts of your past are still with you—
the memories and pain you carry deep inside?

What would it be like
to set them down, even just briefly,
and create space for healing?

Where do you find safety now—
and how can you invite more of it in,
even when the storm rages?

How can you show kindness
to the younger you who survived so much
without the tools to protect yourself?

✧ ECHOES
Held in the Aftermath

Some EMDR sessions crack you open.
Others leave you curled inside yourself—
quiet, blinking,
trying to find gravity again.

This one did both.

That night, I still felt like I was in the basement.
Still dodging objects mid-air.
Still bleeding, even if only inside.

I could see the toaster.
The knives.
The sting of metal on skin.
The way fear rushes in
after the pain—
not the physical kind,
but the ache underneath it.

The kind that lingers
long after the bruises fade.

Hours later, I was on the couch.
Wrapped in a blanket.
Body aching.

The world felt far away.
Like I had been dropped back into the present,
but the gravity hadn't caught up yet.

I tried to eat.
Couldn't.

Tried to speak.
Nothing came out.
Not because I didn't want to—
but because my body hadn't found its breath again.

That's the thing about trauma:
it doesn't just live in the past.
It lives in your breath.
Your jaw.
Your spine.
Your gut.

It shows up when you try to rest—
echoes in the silence
after a session like this.

And yet—
the next morning, I woke up.
Sore. Puffy-eyed. Hollow.

But something was different.

Like my body had heard me.
Like that boy at the bottom of the stairs
had finally been seen.

Not as the problem.
Not as the one who caused the damage—
but as the one who lived through it.
And deserved to.

This is what EMDR can feel like.
Not clarity. Not closure.
Just breath.
Just presence.
Just enough space
between the memory and the shame.

And for now—
that's enough.

I thought about quitting after this session.
Told myself I couldn't keep doing this.
Couldn't keep going back into memories
that still had teeth.

But then I remembered how far
I've already walked through fire
and didn't burn up.

How many times I've sat in that chair—
shaking, unraveling—
and still left whole.

I remembered the boy at the bottom of the stairs—
the one who didn't have anyone.
No therapist. No language.
No name for what was happening.

Now he has me.
He has words.
He has breath.
And he has someone in the room
who doesn't look away.

I remembered the way my therapist sits in the quiet—
not trying to fix it,
just bearing witness
to what was never seen.

And somehow, that makes it safer to keep going.
Not easier. Never easy.
But possible.

This isn't just about pain.
It's about reclamation.

Reclaiming the sound of my own voice.
Reclaiming what my body tried to tell me all along.
Reclaiming the right
to be angry,
to grieve,
to rest.

This session didn't bring resolution.
It didn't patch the hole in my chest.

But it gave me just enough breath
to face another day.
Just enough safety
to hold the memory without becoming it.

And that's what healing looks like sometimes—
just enough.

Not closure.
Not forgetting.
But enough to keep going.

Enough to keep coming back
until the boy doesn't flinch
when the stairs show up in his dreams.

Until he knows he's not going back there alone.

Because this time,
I have someone with me.

She doesn't pull me out—
she meets me there.
Grounded.
Steady.
Like she has her hand on my heart
without ever touching it.

Holding just enough light
for me to see the edges of the storm
 without getting lost inside it.

Just enough breath
for me to remember
I made it out once—
and I can again.

That I am not what happened to me.
That I am not alone
in this remembering.

And that even in the darkest rooms,
healing is still possible—

because someone stayed,
because I stayed,
because we stayed
long enough
to see who I really am.

Chapter Thirteen
The Wall and the Return

EMDR Session
When the Body Seeks Safety in Pain

My therapist walks me into the room.
She asks how I'm doing, how my day's going.
I say,
"It's going good. I feel great today."
She asks,
"Are you ready for EMDR?"
"Yes. Let's go. Let's get it. I'm really feeling the effects, and I'm so
grateful it's helping me."

I sit in the comfy chair across from her.
We talk about how long I've been doing EMDR.
How far I've come.
She asks,
"How do you feel it's working?"
I say,
"It's working very well. I definitely have more in the tank."

I pull out my phone,
scroll to the list—
the memories that still live in me.
I start reading.
There's one I haven't talked about yet.
A time my mom was hurting me.

It feels
heavy.

She hands me the buzzers.
I don't go to my safe place.
I don't enter the storm.
I'm just... in the dark.

Eyes closed.
Buzzers humming.
Silent.

And then—
a wave.
Tears.
Heavy.
Unstoppable.

I'm crying hard, leaning over.
"This is intense," I say.

The storm begins—
but it's different this time.
Slower.
Heavier.
Frightening.

The storm is afraid.
And so am I.

I'm in a memory.
I don't even know what I did wrong.
I just remember... I'm in it.

My mom grabs me by the back of the neck,
screaming,
blaming me for something.
She throws me into the wall.
I hit.
Fall.
Get back up.

My back hurts.
My neck aches.
I'm screaming.
Crying.
I run to her—again.

She grabs me.
Slaps me.

Punches me in the back—near my kidney.
Throws me across the room.
Back into the wall.
Again.

I get up.
Limping.
Crying.
And run back.

She does it again.

The pain is unbearable.
The sadness—
the fear—
the anger—
it's all inside me, all at once.

I look at my therapist,
tears pouring down my face.
I try to speak—
but I can't.
The trauma takes my voice.

Silence.

She asks,
"What do you notice?"

I finally manage,
"Why... why did I keep running back to my mom? When she was
the one hurting me?"

She speaks calmly,
"You were a little boy.
Afraid.
Thrown against a wall.
And your body ran toward the person who was supposed to
protect you.
That's what children do."

I nod,

"That makes sense.
I didn't understand.
My body hurt everywhere—
my back, my arms, my neck.

Every time she threw me,
I still ran back,
like I was saying,
'Stop. Please stop. Hold me. Don't hurt me.'
Like something would change.
But it didn't."

The memory fades.
Darkness.
Stillness.

I'm crying.
So deeply sad.
Minutes pass.

My therapist holds space.
I need that.

I don't know what all these emotions are.
But I know I need to feel them.

Then—
another memory fractures open.

I'm in the kitchen.
I spill a drink.
My brother's at school.
It's just me and my mom.

She yells,
accuses me of doing it on purpose.
I didn't.

She grabs my arm,
drags me down the hall,
throws me into the TV room closet,
slams the door shut.

I hear her slide something heavy across the floor—
a chair?
A trunk?

The door won't open.
There's light under the crack from the TV room.
I slide my fingers through it.

She must've seen—
because she shoves a blanket down,
blocking the light.

Dark.
I'm crying.
I can't breathe.
It feels like the oxygen's running out.

I scream.
Kick the door.
Try everything.

She yells,
"If you break that door, you'll be in more trouble."

Then—nothing.
She walks away.
Back to the kitchen.

I'm alone.
Freaking out.
Desperate for air.
Pushing.
Searching for light.

I don't remember coming out.
I don't know if I passed out or fell asleep.

I tell my therapist,
"I can't remember."

She says gently,
"That's okay. What else comes up?"

I say,
"Yes.
There were so many times.
I was thrown in closets all the time.
I never got used to it."

She says,
"How could anyone get used to that?"

I nod,
"I know.
Sometimes I'd think,
'Well, I'm not being hit—
but I can't breathe.
How do I get out?'"

Sometimes it was the same closet.
Sometimes another.
Some bigger.
Some smaller.

Once I climbed into a trunk for a blanket—just fooling around.
It shut on me.
I freaked out.

It felt just like those closets.
Only tighter.

I didn't think I'd get out.
It felt like forever
until my brother opened the lid.

That memory is fuzzy.
I don't know if my mom shut it.
If she put me in there.
But it scared me.

I think that's why
I have claustrophobia.
Why I hate the dark.

I feel the anger again.

My mom used to say,
"You have a great temper,"
like it was a badge of honor.

When I got mad,
my temper exploded.
Didn't matter how big they were.
I'd fight.

I tell my therapist,
"When I'm angry, it feels good.
Adrenaline rushes through me.
My blood, my muscles, my veins.
I feel unstoppable. Invincible. Indestructible."

But I wanted it to stop.
I wanted to understand
why anger ruled me.

It was the beatings.
The closets.
Being thrown.
Being hit.
Being trapped.

Those moments hardened me.

I used to say,
"I can't take my dad's mental abuse—
but I could take the physical,
because I don't remember it."

But in that session,
with the buzzers,
I realized—

My brain doesn't remember most of it.
But my body does.

My body holds the score.
My body remembers.

I feel so much sadness.

Mentally abused.
Physically abused.
Beaten. Belittled. Betrayed.
Rejected.
Like I was never wanted.

In that room,
with those buzzers,
I'm feeling it all—
grief,
sadness,
a longing for love,
for comfort,
for safety.

And I start to ask,
"How did I become who I am?
How did I raise two beautiful daughters
and create a safe home?"

My therapist looks at me.
She speaks quietly,
"It sounds like you gave them what you didn't have."

I nod,
"You're right. I did."

She isn't naming it for me—
just affirming what I already see.

Her presence.
Her tools.
Her calm.

They guided me through this session—
this fraction of time
that holds a lifetime in my body.

EMDR.
The buzzers.
The process.
They're moving it.

Releasing it.
Organizing it.

I understand EMDR now.
Its power.
Its impact.

Tears fall.
Tears of joy.
Tears of gratitude.

I go to my safe place.
I sit on the bench.
I think about the little boy—
the one thrown into walls.

Part of me is sad.
Wishes I could go back.
Stop it from happening.

But I can't change the past.
I can release the memory.

And I remember—
I survived.

No matter what,
I survived.

I stand in my safe place.
Eyes closed.
Breeze on my skin.
Trees rustling.
River sounds.

I feel grounded.
Grateful.
Confident.
Strong.

I thank myself for surviving.
And it's like the little boy is there beside me,
looking up and saying,

"Thank you."

I say,
"No, thank you.
Thank you for being strong.
For surviving so much pain.
Thank you."

I open my eyes.
Wipe the tears.
Smile.

I say,
"Thank you. Another great session."

My therapist says,
"You did great today.
Thank you for showing up—
for staying with it.
This isn't easy."

🌿 Closing Reflection

This wasn't just a session.
It was a breakthrough.

A deep one.
A core memory unraveling.
A full body response.

Afterward, I felt exhausted—
but not flooded.

It was *strange*—
because for the first time in my life,
I felt grounded in my body
after remembering something horrific.

Usually, those memories take me out.
But this time,
I returned.

I didn't get lost.
I didn't dissociate.
I didn't spiral or crash or go numb for days.

I cried hard.
I shook.
I grieved.
And then—
I stayed.

I stayed in the room.
I stayed in my body.
I stayed with myself.

This is what people don't understand about trauma:
it's not the memory itself that destroys you.
It's how alone you were in it.

How the pain got stuck inside your nervous system
with nowhere to go.

But now—
it has somewhere to go.

This session changed me.
I felt it.
I still feel it.

For the first time since I was a little boy,
I can say—
I am not afraid of my memories anymore.

They're still painful.
But they're not prisons.
Not monsters in the dark.

They are echoes—
held by a body that finally feels safe enough
to let go.

I used to think the goal of therapy was to erase the pain.
Now I know:
the goal is integration.
To *remember and remain.*
To walk back through the fire
and *not disappear.*

This is the moment I returned to myself.

And I'm not leaving again.

❖A Question to Sit With
How can you gently hold the parts of yourself that were hurt,
offering them kindness and patience in the midst of your healing?

✧ ECHOES

When the Armor Stays Down

That night after the session,
I didn't feel numb.
I didn't feel overwhelmed.
Not angry. Not sad.

I felt... refreshed.
Clear.
Like I came home holding something gentle.
A gift.
Not a breakthrough — not that kind —
but something better.
Peace.
Stillness.
A kind of quiet I hadn't met before.

I didn't want to sleep.
I wasn't exhausted.
My body wasn't buzzing or heavy or frozen.

So I went for a walk.
To my favorite park —
the one with the trail that leads to my safe place.

And I walked it.
Light.
Steady.
Like my body belonged to me again.

I didn't need to pick the armor back up.
Didn't even want to.

Even the hard things — the memories, the pain —
they were still there,
but they didn't pull me under.

They felt like part of the landscape now,
not the storm.

I remember the sunlight.
The way it landed on my shoulders.
I remember thinking:
This is new.

I wasn't vibrating anymore.
No deep tremor under my ribs.
No earthquake waiting to start.
No invisible alarm screaming be ready.

I've lived most of my life in the fight.
Not just fight-or-flight —
fight.
The part that pushes through
bleeds through
breaks through.

But on this day,
both fight and flight
let go of me.

And it felt good.
Strange, but good.

I didn't know what to do with the quiet.
Didn't know how to be
without the buzzing in my bones.
But I stayed with it.

I let the trail carry me.

And if you're reading this —
if you've stopped EMDR,
or you're afraid to start,
or it's gotten too loud inside —
I want you to know:

You deserve to heal.
You're not wrong for struggling.
And it's okay to come back.

Even if it's slow.
Even if it hurts.
Even if you don't know where it will lead.

Just... come back.
Keep trying.

Because one day, you might walk out of your trauma
and into a path you've never known.

One where you're not bracing.
Not locked inside the old war.
Not shaking.

Just... healing.
Not broken.
Not fixed.

Just becoming.

⊚ Chapter Fourteen

Before Words: Body Memories of Early
Trauma

EMDR Session
Broken Bones, Silence, and Unspoken Pain

I remember talking with my therapist
before she handed me the buzzers—
about
some of these things that happened to me
before I could really remember.
And I wanted to focus on those times that
happened when I was just a baby,
or when I was three and four—
and that I feel them
but I don't necessarily remember everything—
besides pieces.

And so
she hands me the buzzers.
And I begin.

This time the buzzers feel calm.
They're not as extreme.
I don't feel like I'm entering a storm.
I'm more of an *observer*—
telling the story
of what happened to me.

And I'm trying to connect deeply with it,
but it's hard—
because these memories
are not in my mind.
They're in my body.

So I explain.
What I'm feeling.

What I'm hearing.

I tell her—
There was a time
that I do kind of remember,
but it's still very fuzzy.
I think I was two, maybe three.
And—
I went in my grandmother's room
and I grabbed a bottle.
A bottle of pills.
Her medicine for her MS.

And that's all I remember.
But I remember my family
talking about it.
How my grandfather
came into the room—
because we were at his house visiting—
and he had found me on the floor.
With pills everywhere around me.
I must have ingested half the bottle.
And I was rushed to the hospital
where I got my stomach pumped.

But I don't remember the hospital.
I don't remember my stomach being pumped.
I just remember grabbing the bottle.

I was blamed for that.

I remember being blamed for that
throughout my childhood.

"You get into stuff," my mom would say.
"You don't listen," my dad would say.

And they would remind me—
like the time you took your grandmother's pills
and we had to take you to the hospital
to get your stomach pumped.
You cost us all this money.

You ruined a happy evening.

I feel the buzzers pick up speed.
I'm not quite emotional.
Still observing.
Breathing hard.
Feeling the pain of **guilt and blame**—
but not from the event itself.

I remember another time—
where I felt pain
but I didn't know what had happened.
And I could piece this together
because of pictures,
and again, people in my family talking about it.
My parents blaming me for it.

A time where we had all gotten together
for family photos in a studio—
a professional photographer.

And I guess I was sitting on the floor,
and I didn't want to stand up,
I didn't want to partake—
like most kids do.
I was two.
Maybe three or four.

And my mom—
decided to grab me by my arm
and pull me up as fast as she could.
And **my arm broke.**

I remember the pain,
but I don't remember that night.
But I remember the photos.
And I remember
the *pain of my arm breaking*—

how bad it hurt.

In the photo,
you can tell I'm holding my arm
and I'm crying.
My mom had me *suck it up*
so I could take the photo.

I don't remember going to the doctor
to get my arm fixed.
I don't remember having a cast.
I don't think I ever was taken in
to have a cast.

I think
my mom just wrapped my arm
and let it heal on its own.

I don't remember—
it *feels* like it.
Because my arm,
to this day,
still hurts.
As if it was never properly set.

I remember a time—
me and my brother were playing
at my grandfather's house.
We were jumping on the bed.

And I jumped off.
And when I hit the floor—
I broke my leg.

I remember being in so much pain.
But I don't remember what happened after that—
besides my mom coming downstairs
with my dad.

Saw that I had a broken leg.
I was crying.
And they kept yelling—
"Great. You messed up another night."

They didn't come to me and hold me.
They didn't try to fix my leg.

She yanked me off the ground.
My dad picked me up out of her arms.
They carried me to the van.
And then I don't remember.

I guess I went to the hospital.
Maybe that's when I had a cast.
But I don't remember ever having a cast on my foot.
I just *remember pain*.
I remember being blamed
for breaking my leg.
For goofing off.

I remember a time
I guess I was "so bad"
at my grandparents' house.

We were celebrating New Year's.
I was playing on the piano—
making all this noise.
Screaming. Yelling.

Because no one would listen to me.
I was hungry.
Or I wanted attention.
I was being ignored.

Everyone else was having a good time.
It was loud.

And I remember

my mom grabbing me off the stool
next to the piano—
smacking me on the back of the head,
spanking me,
tossing me down the hall,
telling me *go away.*

And she went back into the party.

I remember
my grandmother rolling down the hallway
in her wheelchair.
She asked if I wanted to sit on her lap
and come be part of the party.
I said "Okay."

She took me back in.

And then my mom yelled—
"You're not supposed to be in here."
And she gave me a spanking.

I don't remember much after that,
but I remember the blame.

And I remember—
that years later
they would remind me
how bad I was
on that New Year's.

And that when I turn 16 years old,
they were going to punish me.

They reminded me every New Year's—
don't forget when you turn 16,
you're going to stay home.
You ruined a New Year's for us.
We owe you payback.

And they'd tell this story
to friends, to family.

To me.

The blame weighed heavy.
Unbearable blame.

Then—
the storm picks up.
I'm feeling emotional.
Angry.
Sad.
Scared.
Afraid.

My body tenses.
She notices.
Gently, she asks,
 "What's coming up for you right now?"

I pause.
Then I say—
"I'm feeling angry. Upset. I'm remembering a time—
a time where the blame was violent."

I had parked my bicycle—
I think I might have been seven—
behind the van.
Didn't know my dad was going to work.
We were just playing outside.

Me and my brother.
Came inside for a drink.
It was hot. Summer.

As I walked back outside—
my dad was leaving.

Right at that moment—
he backed over my bike.

My mom was there saying goodbye.
He stops.
Starts yelling at me.
"Why'd you put your bike behind the van?"
Calling me careless.
Saying I ruin everything.

He peels out.
Runs the bike back over.
Tosses it—
wheels spinning out.
Across the driveway.
Bent. Destroyed.

I'm crying.
My mom grabs my arm.
Grabs my chin.
"Look what you did."
Calls me names.
Slaps me.
Throws me into the gravel.

My brother's standing there.
Says, "It's okay. You can ride my bike."

Then my mom yells—
"No he can't."

She runs into the garage.
Grabs a sledgehammer.
Brings it out.
Looks at me.

"You did this."

She starts smashing his bike.
Handlebars. Rims. Tires.
Pedals. Chain. Frame.
Over and over again.

Until it's bent like mine.

My brother's crying.
"Why did you do this? Why did you put your bike there?"

Now he blames me too.

The sledgehammer lands
just shy of me—
thrown in rage.

She runs back into the house.
We're sitting outside.
My brother's angry.
I'm broken.

The blame.
It sits heavy with me.

I tell my therapist—
"Why did these things have to happen to me? What did I do?"

She holds space.
Gives me time.

I remember—
weeks later
we took my brother
to get a new bike.

He was rewarded.
I wasn't allowed anything.
No toy. No bike.
Just *reminders*—
of what I had done.

In the session,
I'm overwhelmed.
The protector is coming out.

I say—
"I want to hurt them.
I want to take that sledgehammer
and smash their face.
I want to cause pain."

My therapist's voice is calm:
"Just stay with that. What do you notice as you say that?"

"I want to beat them.
I want to break something of theirs.
Squeeze them.
Squeeze the life out of them."

The rage is pouring through me.

And then—
calm.
The buzzers shift.

I say—
"I don't want to.
Because it doesn't solve the problem."

She nods.
"Okay. Tell me more."

"They deserve it.
But it doesn't fix anything.
It just pulls me deeper into the storm with them."

I realize—
healing is happening.
I don't have to hold their chains.
I can walk away.

I'm better than that.
The protector
doesn't need to protect right now.

I thank him.
I forgive him.

We're all together now—
the little boy,
the protector,
and me.

My therapist asks—
**"Notice what you need right now—
does it feel right to stay with it,
or to go to your safe place?"**

I return.
We all return.
The little me.
The protector.
The adult me.

We sit in peace.
We're becoming one.
Tired, but united.

And it's beautiful.

I open my eyes.
Didn't realize I'd been crying.
But the tears came anyway.
Felt good.

I take a deep breath.
Hand her the buzzers.
Smile.

**"Thank you again. I'm so grateful for this moment.
I'm starting to feel gratitude."**

She says,
"You're doing great."

🌿 Closing Reflection

The amount of blame that has been placed on me over the years as a child
sits heavy in the form of trauma.
It still weighs me down.
Especially when I catch myself
in moments where maybe my daughters
have done something—
an accident, a spill at the table—
and before I react, I pause.
I think about me.
I think about them.

And I don't react the way
my parents reacted to me.
Instead, I run to them,
and I say,
"Are you okay?"
"That's okay."
And I clean it up if they spilled it.
I tell them,
"That's okay, we can get another glass."

Or I comfort them,
ask, "What happened?"
I try to listen.
Hear their side.
Let them speak it out.
Let them know I'm not upset.
I'm not mad.
These things happen.

I remember times when my daughters
have fallen off their bikes,
or gotten hurt, scuffed a knee.

Immediately, my body reacts—
anger, frustration.

But I run to them with gentleness.
Calming, healing, nurturing.
I come with love.

But underneath my skin,
I feel the echo of what was done to me—
when I was hurt,
they didn't run to comfort me.
They ran to blame me.
Beat me. Abuse me.

But I run to my kids,
and I hold them.
Say,
"It's going to be okay."
Patch them up,
put them back on their bike,
tell them to go back out there.
Have fun.
Go back to it.

If anything,
this session is teaching me what is stuck inside—
and how to release it.

It is so needed.
Because I don't know
how I would find these tools,
this opportunity,
this safe place,
this space
to sort all this out—
without EMDR.
Without the help of my counselor and therapist.
Without these sessions.
Without them being good at what they do.

❖A Question to Sit With

How might your own body and mind be holding onto old blame
or pain—
and what small act of compassion could you offer yourself today
to begin softening those wounds?

If you were to imagine a safe place within yourself,
what would it look like—
and how could you visit it when the weight feels too heavy?

✧ ECHOES

Blame in the Bones

That night,
after the session,
I felt like my whole body
was buzzing.

But not in the frantic way —
not storm energy.
Just stirred.
Heavy.

Like the memories
had finally been given
a voice
beneath my skin.

I didn't cry right away.
It was deeper than tears.

I felt the blame
still sitting in my bones.
Like old bruises
never treated.

Like broken parts
never set right.

That session was different.
It wasn't just what I remembered —
it was what my body remembered
before I had words.

And somehow,
I let it come.
Didn't fight it.
Didn't shut it down.

I didn't run to distractions.
I didn't numb.
I didn't rage.

Instead —
I went into the sauna.
Let the heat hold me
like a womb.

Let the sweat
drip out
the poison.

Then —
a cold shower.
Not punishment —
but regulation.

Shock to the skin.
Back to my body.

It helped.
I breathed again.

I didn't even know
I needed that.

Later that night,
I sat with the protector.
The part of me
who wanted to destroy
everything that ever hurt us.

I let him speak.
Let him rage.
Let him soften.

I held the boy.
The one who got blamed
for every accident,
every break,

every hurt
he never caused.

And I held myself.
The one who chooses now.
The one who is learning
how to stay.

Stay regulated.
Stay soft.
Stay whole.

No longer the villain
in someone else's story.
No longer the broken kid
to blame.

Just me.

Home in my body.

Safe in my truth.

Healing —

one echo at a time.

Chapter Fifteen

When I Saw Too Much

EMDR Session
The fight that shaped my fear

My therapist hands me the buzzers.
"Today, let's focus on the violence—
the violent part of my trauma.
Things I've seen."

The buzzers start to vibrate.
Left. Right.
My eyes shift.
I drop into the storm.
Bypass my safe place.
I'm there.

My body's on alert.
Breath shallow.
Fight or flight has kicked up.
I'm bracing.
It feels real—
like I'm there again.

She says,
"What do you notice?"
"Just go with that."

My brother was in a fight.
Some kid.
He called his friends—
half the school, it seemed.
Football players.

Big high school guys.
I might've been twelve. Maybe thirteen.

They came right before sunset.
Everyone lined up.
Talking. Waiting.
My parents were there.
That's when I realized—
they were setting up a fight.

Some kid had messed with my brother's car.
He had to be punished.
That was the logic.
Everyone knew what was coming.

I stood there—*frozen*.
My sister on the porch, flapping her arms.
Excited. Laughing.
I stood beside her.
I asked my parents,
"What do I do?"

They handed me a shovel.
"To protect yourself," they said.
Then my brother said,
"Let's go get him."
They called the kid.
Fighting already—through the phone.
My brother said,
"I'll come pick you up. We'll fight here."

They left.
We waited.
My mom said,
"Go hide behind the lawnmower."
So I took my place.
Behind the mower.
Hidden.

My parents told the others—
"Get in position."
In the trees.

In the woods.
In the yard.

Then headlights.
The cars came down the driveway.
My brother.
His friends.
The kid.
Three or four others.

My brother jumped out.
So did the kid.
It was dark.
The garage light.
A distant streetlight
at the top of the driveway.
That's all we had.

They started to fight.
Punches.
More punches.
Back and forth.
Everyone else stayed hidden.

Then the boy looked up the driveway.
"Who is that?" he shouted.
I looked.
Saw the silhouette of my dad—
carrying chains.
A pickaxe in one hand.
Backlit by the streetlamp.
He walked slow.
Toward the boy.

My brother punched him again.
Caught him off guard.
The boy fell.
Then got up.
Ran.
Right past me.

I flinched—thought he was coming at me.

But he ran right past.
Into the backyard.
My brother chased him.
My dad followed.
My mom ran out of the garage—
a hammer in her hand.
I grabbed the shovel.
Followed.

I couldn't run as fast.
When I got around the house—
I saw the boy slip.
He hit a parked car.
Several were back there.
Everyone had come in cars.

He was down.
My brother ran past me.
Kicked him in the head.
His body spun.
No sound.

He tried to rise.
Then the others came—
out of the woods.
Punching.
Kicking.

I couldn't see the boy anymore.
Just fists.
Sounds.
Moaning.
Yelling.

A scream—"Stop!"

I peed myself.
Pooped my pants.
People laughed.
Spit on him.
Kept hitting.
Kept kicking.

Then my dad shoved others off.
My mom grabbed people—
pulled them back.
She grabbed the boy by his hair.
My dad looped a chain around his neck.
Ran a pickaxe handle through it.
Tightened it.
Lifted him.

"You're going to pay," my dad said.
He asked,
"Where's the stuff you took?"
The kid sobbed.
"Please don't hurt me.
Please don't kill me."
My dad:
"Oh, I'm going to."

He dragged him to a tree.
Tied him there.
Used wire.
Wrapped his wrists.
Then he rolled a push mower over.
Tied the wire to the spark plug.

"If you don't talk—
I'll turn this on."
Everyone stood still.
Watching.

Dad:
"Where did you take it?"
The kid:
"I don't know."

My dad pulled the cord.
The engine sparked.
The shock hit.
The kid screamed.
"I don't know! I don't know!"

Another pull.

Another spark.
No engine—just shock.
I was so sad.
So scared.
So confused.

This isn't right, I thought.
This is bad.
But everyone stood there.
No one stopped it.
No one said, "Enough."

My dad punched him.
Pulled the cord again.
More sparks.
The boy sobbed and said,
"I threw it away.
I gave it to someone.
I'll try to get it back."

Another pull.
The mower roared louder.
The boy wailed.

I stood still.
The shovel like lead in my hands.
Heart racing.
I wanted to run.
To scream.
But I stayed.

Because I was scared.
Because this is what happens here.
Because I didn't know any other way.

The boy whimpered,
"I swear—I'll find it."
My dad nodded.
"Better."
Then he let go.
The boy collapsed.
Coughing.

Breathing.

The crowd dispersed.
The fight was over.
But the fear stayed.

I wiped my face.
Looked at the shovel.
Realized—
This is what my world looks like.
And I don't know how to make it stop.

That night, I didn't sleep.
The sounds stayed.
The fear.
The shouting.
The helplessness.
I asked myself—
Why didn't anyone stop it?
Why didn't someone call for help?
Why did they call this justice?

I was too young to understand.
But I felt it.
It buried itself deep.

At school the next day,
whispers trailed behind me.
"Did you see what your brother did?"
"Your dad's a savage."
"Wild fight."

Some laughed.
Some were impressed.
I felt their eyes on me.
Expecting pride.
But all I felt
was *emptiness*.

Teachers knew.
But said nothing.
No one asked, "*Are you okay?*"
No one said, "*I'm sorry.*"
I was left alone.
With the violence.

In my therapist's room,
I say what I'm scared to say.
"I'm so mad."

I remember my dad's warning:
"If you get bullied,
you better fight back.
If you lose—
I'll be the one to finish it."

His voice still echoes—
like thunder.

I think of the skate station.
The teasing.
The mocking.
The moment *the protector* showed up.
I didn't know who he was.
But I felt him.
Brave.
Strong.
I fought.
I won.
Still got punished.

I tell her,
"I wish I could've protected myself
from all that violence.
I wish I didn't see it."

"It's always there," I say.

"Like shadows I can't outrun."
My anger feels like *grief*.
My grief like *shame*.
"I'm not a violent person," I say.
"I don't want to be.
But I was taught this was normal."

She nods, steady.
"That's what you were shown. It helped you survive."

She asks,
"What do you notice when you sit with that?"

I pause.
Then say,
"That maybe I'm not bad.
That I'm actually a good person.
Just... misguided.
They conditioned me to think this way."

She helps me notice the difference—
between what I say
and what I mean.

Back in my safe place.
Eyes closed.
Buzzers in my hands.
The protector is there.

Not fighting—
but listening.
Trying to forgive.
Trying to be seen.

He's in my safe place.
Feeling what I feel.
Allowed.
Accepted.

Letting go.
Softening.

Tears fall.
Gentle.
More than in the memory.
More than in the violence.

My therapist holds the space.
She lets me settle.
Then says softly—
**"Notice your feet on the ground. Take a walk if that helps. Let
your body keep processing—it knows what to do."**

That's my homework.
I whisper,
"Thank you."
Because in that room—
we were doing something real.
And no words could say enough.

🌿 Closing Reflection

This session
dug up what I buried—
The violence.
The fear.
The chaos.

I held the buzzers.
Felt the weight of it.
But I didn't just relive the fight.
I saw the protector.
The part of me
that learned to survive.

He wasn't just angry—
He was trying to keep me safe.

That changed something.
It opened a space
I didn't know was there.
This wasn't about becoming violent.
It was about understanding
why I believed I had to be.

And for the first time,
I saw another way.
Compassion.
Forgiveness.
Peace.

The protector
became more than a fighter.
He became someone
I could love.
Someone I could trust.
And that
made all the difference.

❖A Question to Sit With

In what ways have you learned to protect yourself through anger, silence, or control—
and how might offering compassion to that part of you
create space for healing, softness, and safety?

✧ ECHOES

After "Seeing Violence"

That night, I went home
and I slept.

Not much.
Four hours maybe.
But it was more than before.

I was exhausted—
bone-tired—
but lighter somehow.

Still upset, though.
Not just from what we processed,
but from everything it reminded me of.

All the violence I've seen.
Not just that night.
Not just once.

But again
and again
and again.

Me being hit.
My brother being hit.
Me forced to hit.
My dad fighting his dad.
Fists. Screams. Bruises. Silence.

All of it surfaced.
And I couldn't unsee it.

The images weren't looping anymore—
not like before,
not like film stuck in a projector—
but they were still there.

Still loud.
Still heavy.

And I felt *so sad.*
Sad that this was part of my life.
Sad that my nervous system was built on it.
Sad that *it's in me,*
even when I try to be gentle.

That evening, I ate something.
Watched TV.
Cried a little.
Went to bed early.
Slept again.
Woke up sore but clearer.

The next day, though—
anger.
Everything felt sharp.

Scrolling through social media
I saw people arguing,
fighting,
hurting each other in ways
that felt too familiar.

Every post.
Every headline.
Every raised voice in public
made my chest buzz.

Like my body was looking for a fight
just to prove it was still here.

I started asking questions I couldn't answer:
Why do humans hurt each other like this?
Why do we raise fists before we raise understanding?

I could've shut down.
I almost did.
It would've been easy to go numb—
to distract, dissociate, disappear.

But I didn't.

I let it move through.
Felt it.
Cried again.
Let myself be angry without picking a fight.
Let myself be sad without falling apart.

And most importantly—
I didn't take on more.
Didn't grab someone else's pain
and carry it like it was mine.

I let mine be enough.

That's what this work is teaching me.
To process what's mine.
To stop swallowing what isn't.
To stop pushing it all back down.

Some days, healing looks like crying.
Some days, it looks like sleep.
Or silence.
Or watching birds outside the window
while your chest aches quietly.

Some days, it's just remembering:
Don't block the storm.
Let it pass.
Feel what needs feeling.
And rest.

That's the only way it fades.

⊚ Chapter Sixteen
Kidnapped and Surviving

EMDR Session
Escaping the Worst

I walk into my therapist's office
already knowing what we're going to face.

I sit down.
Posture stiff.
Eyes alert.
Armor on.

I feel younger than I look—
twelve, maybe.
But I'm doubled up.
Twelve and forty-two.
The little boy on the bench.
The man trying to heal him.
Both of us here,
wearing the armor.

She asks,
"Do you want to talk about the kidnapping?
Do you want to process that?"

I nod.
Ask for the buzzers.
She hands them to me.

"Go to your safe place," she says.
"Spend some time there.
Ground.
And when you're ready,
we can begin."

I close my eyes.

Feel the familiar rhythm—
that *low electric hum*
beneath every tremor in my body.
Fight or flight—
always rumbling underneath.

She says,
"We've never really talked about it.
It's come up…
but maybe now it's time.
To stay with it.
To see what's still there."

One summer evening,
I decided to ride to the gas station.

The sun was setting,
but there was still light.

I'd done it a hundred times—
riding half a mile
down a main road
with no sidewalks,
just woods on either side.

Trees thick.
No houses, just empty grass space.
A factory tucked in the shadows on the left—
hidden just before the station.

The streetlights were too far apart
to make a difference.
Dusk blurred the world in gray.

But I was on a mission.
Candy bars.
Ready for summer.
Riding my bike.

Then—
the sound.
A vehicle speeding up behind me.

I didn't understand it at first.
Not until later.

The sliding door of a van.
No voices.
Just the engine
and the sound of the door—
opening fast.

A bag—
over my head.
I'm still pedaling.
Still moving.

Then—
yanked off.
My bike veers,
crashes into the curb,
topples into the grass.

I'm lifted.
Pulled.
Free-falling through the dark.

Hands—
around my chest,
my arms,
my neck.
Multiple people.
I don't know how many.

The van speeds up.
Takes a turn.
My body shifts with the curve.

My legs—
still hanging out the door.

They try to slam it shut—
once,
twice,
each hit higher.

Ankles.
Knees.
Thighs.

Then—
I fall out.

Hit concrete.
Hard.
I roll.

I rip the bag off.
Some kind of trash bag—
I think.

Everything surreal.
I don't know where I am.
Forget why I left the house.
Forget the bike.

All I see is the van
driving away.
Then—
brake lights.

I turn and run.
Toward the gas station lights.
As fast as I've ever run.

Behind me—
tires screech.
The van turns,
reverses,
spins around.

It's coming back.

I leap the ditch.

Face hits dirt.
I crawl up.

Run.
Trip on the curb.
Smack into concrete.

I make it to the parking lot—
under the fluorescent lights.

Hands scraped.
Knees bleeding.

I'm crawling,
then pushing myself up.
Legs barely working.

Everything frantic.
Nothing moving fast enough.

I'm crying.
Screaming.
"Help! Help!
Someone's trying to take me!"

I slam into the door—
it doesn't open.

I'm pushing.
It's a pull door.

I fumble.
Yank it open.

Run inside.
Jump over the counter.

There's a kid behind the register—
barely older than me.

"I'm being kidnapped!
Call 911! Please help!"

I point out the window—

to the van circling the lot.

It loops once.
Twice.
Then stops on the side.

Inside,
the mirror shows it parked in the shadows.
Lights off.
Brake lights glowing.
I can't see who's inside.

The clerk tells me to calm down.
He picks up the phone.

"I'm calling the police."

I grab it from him.
"Please help.
Please help."

And then—
nothing.

I don't remember what happened after that.

No police.
No sirens.
No questions.

Just a blank.

I must've called home.
Somehow.

Next thing I know—
my dad's there.
The van is peeling off.

He throws me in the car.
Doesn't say a word.
An axe on the floor by his feet.

He speeds after them.

Runs red lights.
Follows them
into the night.

They vanish.
We go back.
Pick up my bike.

Still—
he says nothing.

When we get home,
I'm not comforted.
Not hugged.
Not asked if I'm okay.

I'm punished.

Yelled at.
Beaten.
Grounded.

Thrown in my room.
Lights out.
Week-long sentence.

For being out.
For almost being taken.

But it wasn't *almost*.
I was taken.
I fought.
I survived.

And I was punished for it.

We never spoke of it again.

The silence
was heavier than any blow.

No one asked.
No one checked.

No one saw
how terror still shook in my hands,
how fear clung to my skin.

I learned something that day—
pain was mine alone.
No one would carry it for me.
No one would help me out.

I had to survive it
quietly.
Alone.

So I built walls.

Steel thick.
Emotionless.
Impenetrable.

Walls to keep the fear out.
And people, too.

Because no one protected me.
Not then.
Not ever.

Now—
buzzers in hand.
Eyes closed.
Back in that chair.

The room fades.
The fear returns.

My chest tightens.
My body tenses.

Fight or flight
floods me again.

I'm twelve.
Alone.
Terrified.

But this time—
a voice inside me whispers,

You survived.
You're safe now.

The buzzers hum—
soft, rhythmic.

Drawing the terror out.
Breaking through the armor.

Cracks in the walls.
Tiny ones.
But light slips in.

I'm not just the scared boy.
I'm the warrior
who straightened his legs.

The protector
who held on.

The fighter
who made it out.

I breathe.
Slowly.
Deeper.

I'm here now.
Safe.
Not alone.

The weight lifts.
The dark softens.
I open my eyes.

And for the first time,

I see myself—
not just the victim,
but the survivor.

🌿 Closing Reflection

That session marked a turning point—
where fear began to loosen its grip,
and I saw not just the trauma
but the strength it forged.

Surviving that night wasn't just about escape.
It was about reclaiming something
that was always mine—
my voice.
My fight.
My power.

The warrior in me didn't rise with rage.
He rose with *will*.
With *instinct*.
With *hope*.

Healing doesn't erase what happened.
But it softens the ground
so I can walk forward.

One breath at a time.
Toward peace.

❖A Question to Sit With
What part of your story
still lives in your body—
not as weakness,
but as proof
you never stopped surviving?

How might you begin
to honor the fight in you
that's been there
all along?

✧ ECHOES
Where the Memory Belongs

After that session, I went home and cried.
Not a quiet cry.
A breaking-open cry.
The kind that comes from somewhere older than language.

I started seeing things.
Not visions — patterns.
How my trauma is in everything.
How it decides what I do.
How I show up in public.
How much I scan.
How fast I flinch.
How I parent.

I'm so afraid of my daughters being taken.
Especially my youngest.
When she plays in the yard, I have to be out there.
She can't be alone.
She can't walk down the street by herself.

I bought her tracking devices.
Her backpack. Her shoes. Her watch.
At school, I watch the little dot on my phone.
Every move, accounted for.
A part of me still thinks:
If something happens, I'll be close enough to stop it.
That I'm keeping her safe.
But it's not safety.
It's control.
And underneath that—fear.

Even in public, I can't relax.
I never have my back to a crowd.
I scan for exits.
I study people: their shoes, bags, necklaces, the way they walk,
what they eat, what they sound like.

I count the bodies in the room.
I mark the ones who feel off.
I memorize escape plans.

This is how I live.
Every day.
In my head, I'm playing out what-if scenarios.
My daughter goes to get the mail,
and I see
everything.
All the ways she could disappear.
All the ways I could fail her.

But to her?
She's just getting the mail.
She's skipping back, smiling,
talking about the sunshine.
And I smile too—
while sweating inside,
shaking in places no one sees.

She thinks I'm just being her dad.
Protective.
Present.
Fun.
She doesn't know I'm fighting off ghosts in real time.

She knows about bad people.
I've told her enough to make her aware—
not afraid.
She doesn't know about what happened to me.
I never told her I was kidnapped.

But I think about it.
I think about how different things might've been
if someone had prepared me.
If someone had cared.
If I hadn't been told "go on"
with a careless wave
that said more than words ever could.

They knew.
They knew things like that happened.
And they let me go anyway.

That memory cracked something open.
This session did.

I see now—
how much of my life
has been lived from inside fight or flight.
Like I've been armoring myself
for a war that already happened
but never ended.

This work —
EMDR,
my counselor, therapist,
this space —
it's doing something.
It's shifting something.

I didn't know
if I could ever come out of this.
Didn't know what it would feel like.
Didn't expect clarity.
Didn't even expect peace.

The goal wasn't that.

The goal
was to feel.
To remember.
To stay.
To let the memories come,
and finally,
let them go
somewhere they belong.

⑥ Chapter Seventeen
When Cruelty Felt Normal

EMDR Session
Witnessing Harm in the Family Home

I remember walking into the room with my therapist that day—
sitting across from her
and pausing for a moment.
Pausing
to collect myself,
to prepare myself—
to speak things
I'm not proud of.
Things I witnessed.
Things I felt like
I took part in.

This was a tough session
because even though it was trauma,
it felt like I had to own some of it.
And I didn't know
what the storm would be like.

I tell her—
there were times
I watched my mom
put things in my grandfather's drink
to make him sick.
Poison.
Laxatives.
Toxic stuff.

She hands me the buzzers.
She says gently,
"Just bring up the image, and notice what comes."

The buzzers pick up.
Left—right—left—right.
Moving my eyes.
Feeling the vibration.

This time
I feel like I calmly walk into the storm.
Part of me feels like *I am the storm.*

This session feels different.
I'm upset.
I'm emotional—
and then the memories hit.

I remember sitting on the couch
watching my grandfather play cards.
He gets up to use the bathroom.
My mom rushes to the kitchen—
pulls out ant killer.
A brown bottle.
She drops one—
two—
three—
four drops
into his water.
She stirs it.
The water's cloudy
but still looks drinkable.

She hides the bottle.
Runs to sit back down.
Giggles.
Tells me to stay quiet.

My grandfather returns,
sits back at the table.
Unaware.
He couldn't smell or taste—
he lost those senses due to a health injury.

He lifts his glass.
Takes a sip.

Then a bigger sip.
Keeps playing.

I stare at the water.
At him.
When will it hit?
Is he going to die?

I was scared.
I loved him.
But my mom
had trained me
to see him as the enemy.
To believe
he was the problem—
not me.

And so I sat there.
Part of it.
Silent.
Guilty.

How can you love someone
and watch them be poisoned—
and not say anything?

I'm crying.
I'm destroyed.
I'm afraid.
I say this out loud
for the first time.
I don't think I've ever told anyone
until now.

But here I am
with my therapist—
holding the buzzers—
confessing trauma.
Confessing guilt.
Confessing complicity.

Later that night,

he was sick.
Really sick.
Throwing up.
Stuck in the bathroom.
He said he must've caught something.

But *I knew.*
I knew exactly what it was.
And I felt
so
terrible.

There was another time—
same pattern.
He leaves the table.
My mom pours laxatives into his drink.
She tells me,
"It's just laxatives. He deserves it. He's not good to us."

We had moved in
to help him take care of my grandmother.
She had MS.
It was supposed to be a new beginning.

But it didn't feel like one.
Not with things like this happening.
The trauma
took a new form
in that house.

He never did anything—
nothing to deserve this.
But my mom was convincing.
And I was afraid.
Afraid if I said something,
if I disobeyed,
she'd turn it on me.
Poison me.

Who could I trust anymore?
If she could do that to him,
what else was she capable of?

Was she doing it to my sister, too?

My sister was disabled.
She wouldn't know if her drink was altered.
She wouldn't know if her food wasn't safe.

My mind raced.
I was terrified.

My grandfather kept getting sick.
Kept booking doctor's appointments.
Kept getting brushed off—
"He must've caught a bug."

No one checked him for poison.
He never suspected.

Another time—
summer.
The patio.
Family over.
It seemed like a normal day.
He was cleaning up.
Preparing to play cards with a friend.

My mom took his glass,
walked downstairs,
and grabbed rat poison
from the laundry room.

She added it to his tea.
Stirred.
Put it back.

No one noticed.
No one knew.
He drank it.
Got very sick.
Stayed in bed for days.
No one checked on him.
No one cared.

How could we live in that house,
treat each other like this—
ignore each other in such a small space—
and *I... just witness it all?*

Over the years,
I started believing my mom.
Believing maybe he was bad.
Especially after he kicked us out.

Maybe he knew he was being poisoned.
Maybe he caught on.

It all came to a head
in that last fight
between him and my dad.
Then we were gone.
Forced to move out.

A few months after we moved out,
my dad told me—
"You should sneak in,
type this command
on your grandfather's computer.
It will wipe everything."

They praised me.
Called me a genius.

I knew what the prompt did.
It would format the entire computer.
Erase everything.

One day,
I watched my grandfather drive off
to the nursing home to see my grandmother.
She had to go to the nursing home when we moved out.
She needed 24 hour care.

I told my friend across the street,
"I'm going back into my old house.
Be my lookout."

He agreed.
We ran over.
Found a window unlocked.
I climbed through.
Went straight to the computer.
Typed the code.
Paused.
Should I really do this?
But I did.
Hit enter.
Watched it all erase.
Gone.

Later that night,
my dad asked me,
"Did you do it?"
I said yes.
They said,
"Good job."

And I felt—
for once—
like *I wasn't the bad one.*
But I was.

I feel so ashamed.

My therapist speaks, gently,
"What are you noticing right now?"

I start crying again.
Tears falling fast.
I'm overwhelmed.

Because I let it happen.
Because I knew.

Because years later,
after I emancipated myself,
my grandfather took me back in.
He became my guardian
until I could be my own.

We rebuilt.
Slowly.
Quietly.
Over dinners.

He once told me,
*"I've been working on our family genealogy for years—on my
computer—*
but then one day, it just erased itself."

I nearly collapsed inside.
I had done that.
Wiped years of work.
Gone
in seconds.

"Did you ever get it back?" I asked.
He said,
*"No. I rebuilt it at the church. It's more secure now. It means even
more."*

He didn't blame me.
Didn't curse the computer.
He just started again.
Rebuilt.
Had purpose.

And I cried in that room with my therapist.
I wish I was as strong as he was.
I wish
I had talked to him more.
Stopped those things.
Warned him.

Did it affect his health?
Shorten his life?
Was I part of that?

I'm grieving.
Ashamed.
But beginning to understand—
It wasn't my fault.

I was a kid.

My therapist says, calmly,
**"You were young. And it sounds like you were doing your best
to stay safe."**

Her words
cut through
and comfort me.

I return to my safe place.
Breathe.
Look around.
I feel lighter.
Like I let something go.
Owned it.
Released it.

Yes—
I formatted the computer.
But I was 14.
Maybe 15.
And I believed
I was doing what was right.
I didn't know.

And I know
my grandfather
would forgive me.

The buzzers stop.
I open my eyes.
Tears on my cheeks.
I hand them back.

I smile at my therapist.
"Thank you."
She nods.
"You're welcome."

I wipe my face.
In awe

of what EMDR is doing for me.
This process—
it's one of the many things
saving me.

🌿 Closing Reflection

That session
helped me overcome
years of guilt
for what I witnessed,
and what I did
to my grandfather.

There were things I didn't share in the session.
But the weight—
was still there.

Like the money I used to take
from his wallet.
I'd take a $20 bill.
Sometimes I'd put it back
after I got paid.
Sometimes I'd return more—
like it earned interest.

It started out feeling like borrowing.
But it wasn't.
I saw my brother do it once.
He told me,
"Don't ever do this."
But I did.

My grandfather knew.
He always knew how much he had.
Every bill.
Every coin.
He knew.
And I think
he just prayed for me.
That I'd figure it out.
That I'd grow up.

He never confronted me.
Never made me feel small.
He just kept loving me.
Quietly.
Powerfully.

And now—
I forgive myself.
This session showed me
that I don't have to carry this weight forever.
I can own it
without letting it crush me.

These memories

are reminders

of how far I've come.

And that,

to me,

is powerful.

❖A Question to Sit With
What part of your story
still holds the weight of silence,
guilt,
or complicity—
and are you ready
to meet that younger version of yourself
with compassion
instead of blame?

✧ ECHOES
What I Choose to Keep

That evening, when I got home,
I talked to my wife about it.

I've told her before
about stealing from my grandfather—
but this time I brought up how
my mom used to poison him.

She didn't even blink.
She just said,
"That sounds like your mom."

No judgment.
She didn't look at me like I had a part in it.
She didn't question it.
She knew that was all my mom.
She felt bad for me.
She hugged me.
We sat there talking about my grandfather—
the good times.
Who he was.

And I didn't feel guilty anymore.

I felt proud.
Proud of who he was.
Proud that I built something new with him later in life.
Proud that I tried to make it right.
That I did everything I could.

This session didn't break me.
The next day,
I just felt... normal.

And you're going to have days like that.

When you're in EMDR,
there will be days where the world crushes you.
Where everything feels sharp and unstable.
Where you cry.
Where you want to sleep,
hide,
numb out,
curl up,
run away.

There will be days
you don't want to be touched.
And days where you crave closeness—
a hug,
a friend,
a distraction,
something warm and alive.

There will be days
that feel numb.
And days that feel
strangely,
beautifully,
normal.
Like you never even had a session the day before.

That's when I think healing starts to land.

This one felt like that.
Like release.
Like healing.
And I'm grateful.

Later,
I told my youngest daughter about him—
who he was,
what he loved,
how cool he was.
I told her stories.
The good ones.
The real ones.

And it felt so good.
It felt normal.

Like I had a childhood.
Like I had adventures.
Like I had a grandfather who took me on everyday
ordinary
beautiful things.

And that's how she sees it now.

I'm not rewriting the past.
I'm just choosing what I want to hold.
What I want to pass down.

Not to erase the pain—
but to carry the love,
too.

⑥ For Trauma Survivors

Author's Note: A Gentle Warning and an Offering
Chapter Eighteen contains graphic depictions of childhood physical abuse, sibling violence, and intense emotional rage. Please honor your pace as you read. If at any point this becomes too much, it's okay to pause. It's okay to come back later—or not at all.

I wrote this to name the unspeakable. To give shape to the chaos I carried in silence.

If you've lived through something similar, I hope this chapter reminds you that you are not alone, and that your pain is not too much. You deserve to be witnessed. You deserve to heal. You deserve to be safe.

Breathe as you read.
You are allowed to feel everything.

⑥ For EMDR Therapists & Counselors

A Note to the Ones Who Hold the Storm
To the clinicians who bear witness to unspeakable pain—
This chapter is for you.

Not to place you on a pedestal, but to reflect back what real trauma-informed presence can make possible.
You'll find no saviorism here.
Just steady ground, sacred silence, and a client brave enough to bring the beast into the room.

You don't speak much in these pages.
But your care is unmistakable.
Thank you for showing us what it means to hold space for rage without fear, and for grief without trying to fix it.
This healing couldn't have happened without that kind of presence.

Chapter Eighteen
Caught in Violence: Brothers and Beatings

EMDR Session
Fighting for Survival in a House of Pain

Sitting across from my therapist,
she hands me the buzzers.
I enter my safe place.

I'm calm today.
I feel stronger.
More steady.
Maybe it's healing.
Maybe it's hope.

The buzzers begin.
I close my eyes.
I feel trust here—
in this space,
with her.

I don't feel as exposed sharing my story.
Even if the tears come—
and they always do—
I won't hold them back.

Not this time.
Not anymore.

I want to stay open.
To let EMDR do its work.
To let the waves crash through me
instead of bracing against them.

My therapist doesn't tell me where to go.
She's silent—
holding space.

And that silence…
it speaks.

Before I can even wonder where we'll go—

a memory.
A rupture.
The storm pulls me under.

I remember how my mom used to beat me and my brother.

Back then, I didn't understand.
I thought it was because we were bad.
That we deserved it.

I thought this was just
how kids got disciplined.
Other kids got spanked—
this was the same, right?

I don't even remember what we did wrong.
Maybe something outside.
Maybe something she saw through the window.
But she called us in.

She sat on a chair in the TV room.
She had my brother lean over her right knee.
Then me over her left.

We were back to back—
I couldn't see him.

Then came the pain.

Not a spanking.
Not a swat.

But
pain.

Sharp.
Relentless.
All over—

my back,
my ribs,
my kidneys,
my spine,
my elbow.

A board.
It had to be a board.
I couldn't see it—
but I could feel it.

I screamed.

My brother yelled:
"No, don't do it!"

Then he was hit.

Back and forth.
Me, then him.
Over and over.

We screamed
until the screams ran out.
I couldn't cry anymore.
Couldn't breathe.
Couldn't think.

The pain became
numb.

I stared at the floor.
Tears dropping onto the carpet.

Until she threw us off her knees.
We hit the ground.

She walked out.

My brother tried to crawl to our room.
I couldn't move.

My arm throbbed.
My back—gone.
I watched his shirt ride up
as he crawled away.

His skin—
red like fire.

I didn't want to know what mine looked like.

Back in the room,
I'm sobbing.
Trying to breathe.

I feel like I'm hyperventilating.
I'm shaking.

Then comes the rage.

I want her to feel it.
The pain.
The board.
Every hit.

I want to give it back.
Break it across her back.
Make her scream the way we did.

I tell my therapist.
I say the violent things.

I'm the lion—
snarling.
Foaming.
Feral.

I want revenge.

For what she did to me.
To him.

This isn't just in my mind—
it lives in my body.
In my fists.
In my breath.

I cry again.

My therapist holds the silence.

I clutch the buzzers,
so tight I worry I'll crush them.

I feel shame.

I'm afraid—
that I'll scare her.
That I'll ruin the room with this rage.
That I'll become
too much.

But I know she can handle it.
She's trained for this.
This space is for this.

Still,
part of me wants to hide.

Because when I'm this angry,
even my wife turns away.

She doesn't see someone who's hurt—
she sees the beast.

So I see him too.

I believe I'm bad.
Because of this.

My therapist grounds me.

"These aren't who you are.

They're parts of you shaped by trauma.
What do you notice?
Just go with that."

Another memory hits.

Flashes.
Fury.
Fear.

Me and my brother—
fighting like kids do.

But she was fed up.
Maybe she was on the phone.
Maybe she didn't have it in her
to beat us again.

So she tried something new.

She grabbed us both.
Dragged us by the arms.
Threw us in the bedroom.

Screamed:

**"Fight each other to the death.
Only one of you comes out alive.
If you're both alive when I come back,
I'll handle it myself."**

And slammed the door.

Me and my brother—
silent.
Terrified.

Looking at each other.
Are we really supposed to…?

We ran into each other's arms.
Sobbing.

"I don't want to hurt you."
"I don't want to kill you."

What do we do?

We started throwing stuff around—
making it sound like we were fighting.

We whispered plans.

Who goes?
Who lives?
Who dies?

He said,

"You're older.
You protect us.
You can't die."

I said,

"You're younger.
You have more life left.
You can't go first."

Back and forth.

Plotting.
Surviving.

Two kids
trying to outsmart death
inside their bedroom.

In the therapy room—
I collapse inward.

I feel like I'm lying on the floor,
but I'm still in the chair.

My tears are stuck
in my chest.
In my throat.

Numb.

I think about my brother.
What if we had done it?
What if we had chosen?
What if we had believed her?

This moment—
shattered.
Frozen in my body.

I was a child.
I didn't even know how to kill someone.

Then she came back.
Opened the door in a rage:

"You couldn't do it?"

She grabbed my brother.
Ran.
Slammed the door behind her.

I froze.

I heard yelling.
Another door slam.
They were outside.

I sat in that room,
alone,
for almost an hour.

Quiet sobs.
Watching the window.

Waiting.

Where are they?
Is he okay?
Is she coming back?

Everything felt thick.
Heavy.

Time stopped.

I held my knees.
Held my breath.

The shadows in the room grew long.

I didn't move.
Didn't speak.
Couldn't.

Now, here.

Still.

The buzzers hum.
Slower.
Steadier.

I return to my safe place.

I breathe.

In…
Out…

I open my eyes.

Hand the buzzers back.

Silence.
But it feels like
safety.

I look around the room—
books, diagrams,
soft lighting,
my therapist's quiet presence.

How did I get here?

To a place where pain
is allowed to exist—
without punishment.

Where truth
can be spoken—
without shame.

Tears fall again.
But this time,
they feel like
relief.

🌿 Closing Reflection

This was one of the hardest sessions I've ever faced.
But my therapist stayed steady—
holding the container,
letting EMDR guide the current,
letting me break open without falling apart.

Here, I could finally name the unspeakable.
Not to be fixed.
Not to be silenced.

Just to be seen.

This is the work.
This is the transformation.

The body trembles,
the rage surfaces,
and something shifts.

I believe this was a turning point.
A crack in the wall
where the light began to pour in.

And for that,
I am deeply gratefull.

❖A Question to Sit With
What part of your story feels the most dangerous to name—
and what might happen
if you let someone witness it
without turning away?

✧ ECHOES
The Stillness Between Storms

That day I went home
and crashed.

Slept the rest of the day.
Fogged out.
Curled up on the couch —
not wanting to be touched,
not wanting to talk,
not wanting to eat.

Just
close my eyes.
Sink.
Drop into the quiet.

And as I slept,
I fell deeper.
Deeper than I have in a long time.

I think it was because
I knew I was safe.
This house.
The home me and my wife built.
The family we're still building.

Safe.

I knew my wife would let me rest.
My daughter would, too.
No one needed anything from me.
I could just
be.

This wasn't like the other sessions.
It didn't feel like an EMDR hangover.

It felt like
rest.
Like I had emptied something out
and now
I just needed time
to refill.

I slept deep that night.
And the next day,
I slept in.

Woke up slow.
Ate something.

Still quiet.
Still heavy.

Not able to focus.
Not wanting to be touched.
Not ready to talk.

The session replayed in my head
again and again.

The beats of it.
The feelings.

Sadness.
Loss.
The beatings.
Betrayal.
Guilt.

But also—
something else.

A pull.

Not dread.
Not fear.

Just this steady
undeniable
urge:

I want to go back.
I want to keep healing.

Not because it feels good.
It doesn't.

Not yet.
Maybe pieces of it.
But mostly,
it feels like release.

And that's enough.

That week,
I stayed quiet.

Didn't have much to say.
Just watched.
Listened.
Let myself drift.

But slowly—
over days,
not hours—

I started coming back.

Piece by piece.
Breath by breath.

Until I felt myself
again.

Refreshed.
Grounded.
Strong.

Ready to go back in.

To face the storm again.
Not just survive it—

but rewrite it.
Reclaim it.
Name it.
Let it go.

Find healing.
One session at a time.

A Note Before the Poem

There are moments in trauma work that mark the shift —
when something long carried begins to lift.

The poem on the next page marks one of those moments.

The poem on the next page was a milestone in my healing.
It was written and given to my EMDR therapist as a way to honor
what we had walked through together:
the work, the pain, the presence, and the transformation.

She read it out loud in the room —
her voice steady,
my hands shaking.

It was the first time I felt the truth of what we'd done together settle in
my body:

I wasn't broken. I was becoming.

And I hadn't done it alone.

She Sat With Me in the Storm
For Fay

I came to you clawed and cornered—
a lion in survival stance,
not by choice,
but by necessity.
Teeth bared,
heart barricaded,
rage in my throat
like a second heartbeat.
I wasn't fierce.
I was fighting.
Fighting to be seen
beneath the ruin.

There was thunder under my skin,
a storm too big for words—
grief that howled,
rage that tore through rooms
before I even knew it was sorrow.
It was chaos,
unclaimed and unnamed.
And you—
you didn't flinch.

You didn't try to tame it.
You sat.
You stayed.
You listened
like the storm was sacred.

The tappers buzzed—
left, right, left—
a rhythm like footsteps
toward the places I swore
I'd never go again.

My eyes moved,
but it was my soul
that broke into those locked rooms.

We went back.
To the moment the light went out.
To the silence that wasn't peace.
To the breath that got stolen.
And you didn't turn away.
You didn't name it for me.
You held space
so I could finally name it myself.

Afterward, I would sleep—
deep, bone-heavy sleep.
Not weakness.
Waking death leaving my body.
Grief-sleep,
the kind that only comes
when the war inside
has finally paused.

You helped me lay the weight down.
Not with force—
with presence.
You helped me peel off armor
I forgot I was wearing.
You saw the warrior in the child,
the child in the warrior.
You honored both.

You didn't just listen.
You anchored the room
when I unraveled.
When I roared.
When I wept
with my whole body.
When I disappeared
into memories
I didn't invite.

You didn't rescue me.
You witnessed me.
You reminded me
I wasn't beyond repair.
You reminded me
healing wasn't a betrayal
of what I'd survived.

Each time I walk through that door,
I gather another piece of myself.
And no—
I am not done.
But I am becoming.

I am grateful.
For the storm.
For the silence.
For your fierce compassion.
For the way you sat with me—
not to fix me,
but to find me.

And maybe most of all—
I'm grateful you walked your own fire first.
That you braved your own storms
and chose to rise.
Because it was your truth,
your healing,
your EMDR journey,
that lit the path I couldn't see.
Without your courage
to live what you now give,
I may never have found mine.

The fire didn't end me.
And you didn't leave me in it.

— Zebulon Thomas

To the Ones Still Standing

We've all been through things.
Every one of us carries a story.
Some of us hold the weight of what we've lived through.
Some have endured what feels impossible to speak aloud.

But if you're reading this —
you made it.

You're a survivor.
A trauma survivor.

I want you to pause —
really pause —
and take that in.

Your story.
And the future that's still possible for you.

Because healing isn't just about what you survived.
It's about what you choose to do with it.

And if you notice tears in your eyes right now —
Tears for what you've survived,
for what that younger version of you endured —

Let them fall.

Let them hit the page if they need to.
I wish I could be there to hold you,
but in these words, I am.

You are not alone.

Your tears are now part of this book.
You've folded your pain into these pages with mine.

You're on the right path —
because you're still here.
Because you're reading this.
Because some part of you still wants more.

So keep going.

I have so much love for you —
for the little boy or girl inside you who is crying right now,
who waited so long to be seen,
who deserves every ounce of compassion and care.

Maybe you'll go on to change the world.
Or maybe you'll change just one life.
Maybe your story will reach one person —
and maybe that's enough.

You don't have to be the best.
You don't have to be famous, or wealthy, or historic.
You don't have to fix everything that broke you.

If your survival gives someone else a reason to hold on —
That is sacred.
That is enough.

I believe in turning pain into power.
In transforming the mess into the message.

We did not ask for the trauma.
We didn't choose the violence, the chaos, the losses we carry.
We didn't know how to survive it.

And yet —
Here we are.

If you're still breathing, still reading,
I believe you're here for a reason.
Maybe you don't know what that reason is yet.
That's okay.

Because on the other side of healing,
purpose doesn't need to be chased.
It finds you.

It rises inside you
and pulls you forward.

That's what happened to me.

I wrote this book to honor the ones who helped me get here.
To honor my counselor and therapist.
To honor the work we did in EMDR.
To honor EMDR therapy itself.

To honor the little boy on the bench —
the protector inside me who never stopped watching.
Never stopped fighting.
Never stopped hoping.

And I wrote this to honor myself.

For surviving.
For showing up.
For fighting my way through when I had nothing left.

I wrote this from a place of love —
a love that I didn't always believe existed.

The kind that finds its way into your chest
when faith begins to flicker through the cracks.

The kind that reminds you:
You were never as alone as you felt.

There were prayers whispered over me that I never asked for.
And now, I carry gratitude for every single one.

I could not have arrived here —
at peace, with this clarity —
without two extraordinary souls.

Two trauma survivors who chose to heal.
Who went back to school.
Who stayed up late, studied hard,
and gave their lives to this work.

Their purpose pulled them —
all the way into that counseling room,
and eventually, into mine.

I walked in wearing armor.
Teeth bared.
Exhausted.
Hopeless.

But somewhere inside, something small —
something ember-bright —
still believed healing might be possible.

And when she handed me those buzzers,
I knew something was about to shift.

I could never have predicted how far that healing would go.
Or how much freedom, clarity, forgiveness,
and grief I'd come to know because of it.

It wasn't just the clinical tools that saved me.
It was who they were.

Because for someone like me —
someone with trauma rooted in violence, silence, and survival —
textbook strategies only go so far.

What saved me was something deeper.
Something real.

They held space when I couldn't hold myself.
They created safety where none had ever existed.

They brought their full humanity into the room —
and met mine there.

Their wisdom.
Their lived experience.
Their ability to see what others couldn't —
that's what helped me see myself.

And I believe, with everything in me:
That's what saved my life.

The Life I Was Never Supposed to Have

Even though my life began in abuse and trauma—even though I endured so much—I survived. Somehow, I found a way to get back up. I pushed through. And not only did I create a better life for myself, I designed the one I wanted.

To others, the things I've done might seem impossible. If I had told you years ago what I planned to do with my life, you might've said, *That's never going to happen. That's impossible.* And honestly? At times, I didn't believe it myself. I was just trying to survive. But even then, I had a small vision—one that grew over time. A hope. A hunger. A relentless obsession that I could turn my pain into something powerful. Something magical. Something meaningful.

That ambition—yes, often fueled by trauma, by fight-or-flight—gave me more than survival. It gave me tools. A mindset. A raw set of instincts that helped me carve a path where none existed. I taught myself things no one else could teach me. I developed a distinct voice in filmmaking, photography, writing, coaching, and live events. And without chasing anyone, my work began attracting the attention of some of the most respected brands, entrepreneurs, and public figures in the world.

I didn't run to them—I stayed focused on what I was building. On what I needed to build to survive. These weren't just passions; they were tools. Each skill became a vehicle—something that could carry me from the streets into classrooms, boardrooms, studios, and stages.

From a street kid to someone walking into schools, helping students learn how to survive, how to recognize danger, how to stay off drugs —or how to get off them. I've been hired by major companies, global brands, and entrepreneurs as a lead strategist, personal advisor, and head of productions. All without a degree—just real-world experience, scars turned into skillsets, and a proven track record of transformation.

I became a tool that helped others achieve their missions. A puzzle piece that fit into their passions, their projects, their businesses—helping them reach goals in record time. And the success I've created for myself and others? It's beyond what I ever imagined. And it's still unfolding.

But this kind of talent—this kind of path—comes with its own risks. It demands discipline. It requires vigilance. I've had to stand guard at the edge of my mind, where my brilliance and my deepest wounds live side by side. That's where the protector in me still shows up—especially in high-profile spaces where harm can still hide in plain sight. Even there, he's watching. Still keeping me safe.

Now, with this new view of my trauma—with healing, clarity, and purpose—I'm more guided than I've ever been. And the energy I once gave away to everyone else—the people, the projects, the billion-dollar brands—I'm giving that same level of love and focus back to *me*. Only now, the purpose is deeper. It pulls harder. It leads with something sacred.

So I surrender to it. I say,
Take me where you want me to go.
Put me where I need to be.

And this book?
It's just the beginning.

To the Ones Who Sit Across From Us

You see us before we even speak.
You watch the shift in our shoulders, the tremble in our breath.
You catch the words we don't say — and you stay.

You don't run from the stories.
You don't fix what can't be fixed.
You sit with it.
With us.

That takes something rare.
Not just training, not just hours in a classroom.
It takes a nervous system that can hold someone else's storm,
without being pulled under.

I know you've had your own healing to do —
maybe that's why you chose this path.
Maybe EMDR saved you too.
Maybe you still carry echoes of other sessions, other clients,
the weight of it all stored somewhere behind your eyes.

You keep showing up.
You learn new tools.
You adapt when one method doesn't work.
You trust the client, even when we've forgotten how to trust ourselves.

You were the first safe person I ever met.

The space you made —
soft chair, weighted blanket, quiet room,
the steadiness of your voice —
was a place I didn't know I needed until I found it.

And now I carry it with me.

To every therapist, counselor, social worker, and healer:
Thank you for learning this work.
Thank you for staying with it.
Thank you for showing us how to return to ourselves —
gently, one breath, one session, one memory at a time.

Please don't stop.
We need you more than we know how to say.

— Zebulon Thomas

The Quiet Triumph: After the Storm

I used to think healing meant forgetting.

That if the trauma no longer screamed inside my chest, maybe it was gone.

But healing didn't take the memories away.
It didn't undo what happened.
It didn't let me bypass the pain.

What it gave me—slowly, relentlessly—was the ability to stay.
To remain present in my own skin.
To sit with a feeling and not run.
To witness my past without becoming it.

That's the miracle EMDR gave me.
Not *erasure*—
But *integration*.

There was a moment—months into the process—when I realized the shaking had stopped.
The storm in my body that had raged since childhood had finally stilled.

I didn't know it could.
I didn't believe it would.
But it did.

And in that stillness, I found something that had always been waiting:
Freedom.

The freedom to choose how I respond.
The freedom to rest.
The freedom to live without flinching at every sound, face, or memory.

To the EMDR therapists reading this,

I want to say this plainly:

The work you do is often unseen.

You carry the storms your clients don't speak about after the session ends.

You witness the victories no one shares.

You hold space for those who return—and for those who leave, sometimes without warning.

It's heartbreaking when someone stops coming back.
When you can't reach them anymore.
When you watch from the sidelines, hoping they'll return when they're ready.

But I want you to know this—

If you save one person, it's all worth it.

I was that one person for my therapist.

I am honored to have survived—not only for myself but for her.

Together, we faced the storm.
Together, we did the hardest work.

That quiet triumph—the slow reclaiming of peace—is a testament to your dedication, your skill, and your belief in the impossible.

You give us back our lives when we think they are lost forever.

To the survivor reading this—whether you've just started, are mid-journey, or are deep in the aftermath:

I see you.
I honor you.
And I promise you—

There is life beyond survival.
There is light after the shaking.

Keep going.
Give yourself time.

And when the storm returns, *as it sometimes will—*

Remember you are no longer alone inside of it.

You have the tools.
You have the space.
And maybe now... you even have the peace.

"I didn't run from the darkness. I sat in it long enough to become the light."

"When I was taken, I didn't lose myself. I buried myself deep enough to survive—and strong enough to come back for me."

"Every time I shattered, I met a piece of myself I hadn't held yet."

"EMDR didn't erase the past. It handed me back the pieces and said, 'Here—make something new.'"

"I lived most of my life in fight or flight—bracing, running, surviving. But I am no longer just surviving. I stepped out of that fire not to escape it, but to carry light to those still inside."

— Zebulon Thomas

Printed in Dunstable, United Kingdom